The First-Year Experiences of Successful Superintendents

Kerry L. Roberts, Sid T. Womack,

Shellie L. Hanna

ROWMAN & LITTLEFIELD EDUCATION
A division of
ROWMAN & LITTLEFIELD PUBLISHERS, INC.
Lanham • New York • Toronto • Plymouth, UK

Published by Rowman & Littlefield Education
A division of Rowman & Littlefield Publishers, Inc.
A wholly owned subsidiary of The Rowman & Littlefield Publishing Group, Inc.
4501 Forbes Boulevard, Suite 200, Lanham, Maryland 20706
www.rowman.com

10 Thornbury Road, Plymouth PL6 7PP, United Kingdom

British Library Cataloguing in Publication Information Available

Library of Congress Cataloging-in-Publication Data

Roberts, Kerry.
The first-year experiences of successful superintendents / Kerry Roberts, Shellie L. Hanna, and Sid T.
Womack.
p. cm.
"Published in partnership with the American Association of School Administrators."
Includes bibliographical references and index.
ISBN 978-1-61048-708-5 (cloth : alk. paper) -- ISBN 978-1-61048-709-2 (pbk. : alk. paper) -- ISBN
978-1-61048-710-8 (electronic)
1. First year school superintendents--United States. 2. Educational leadership--United States. I. Hanna, Shellie L. II. Womack, Sid T. III. American Association of School Administrators. IV. Title.
LB2831.72.R64 2012
371.2'011--dc23
2011051122

The paper used in this publication meets the minimum requirements of American National
Standard for Information Sciences Permanence of Paper for Printed Library Materials,
ANSI/NISO Z39.48-1992.

Printed in the United States of America

Table of Contents

Your Authors

Kerry L. Roberts has been in educational leadership for over twenty-five years. He came from a background in classroom teaching and coaching beginning in 1976, when he taught business, math, and science and coached basketball in the state of Washington. He took his first administrative job in 1983 at a private school in St. Louis, as a superintendent/principal. In 1985 he left the private school and went to work for his brother, Rev. Del Roberts, as a business director at Grace Community Church in Englewood, Colorado. He returned to education in 1986 when he accepted a K–12 principal position in Colorado. From Colorado, he moved to Broken Arrow, Oklahoma, where he worked under Dr. Clarence Oliver, Jr. He has worked as a superintendent in Oklahoma, Kansas, and Minnesota.

His first superintendent position was in Oklahoma in 1992. He has a bachelor's degree from Washington State University in business administration (accounting) and a master's degree from Whitworth University in school administration. He completed his PhD in 1983 at Washington State University with a major in school administration and a minor in tests and measurements. Dr. Roberts is currently an assistant professor of educational leadership at Stephen F. Austin State University, Nacogdoches, Texas. He has presented at local, state, and national conferences on issues dealing with school administration.

Shellie Hanna has been in education since 1992. After completing a degree in history and political science in 1988 and completing teacher-education certification in 1990 at Arkansas Tech University, she added an Arkansas English licensure the following year. Dr. Hanna taught social studies in the Russellville School district in Arkansas for four years. She later completed a master's degree in health and physical education at Arkansas Tech in

2002. She began teaching part-time in 1999 and full-time in 2003 at Arkansas Tech and recently completed her doctorate in educational leadership at Oral Roberts University in Tulsa, Oklahoma, in May 2009.

Dr. Hanna is a recognized leader for health and fitness on the Arkansas Tech University campus. She directs Tech Fit, a fitness center that serves over a thousand students and faculty; manages a team of ten–fifteeen employees; and teaches courses in wellness science, physical education, and physical fitness. Dr. Hanna also performs presentations at local, state, and national levels that deal with both teaching strategies and physical-fitness issues. She also teaches fitness classes for a local fitness center and is active in volunteerism in both her community and church.

Sid T. Womack has been in education for thirty-eight years. He began teaching as a band director in 1972 in Trinity, Texas, after completing a bachelor of music education degree at Abilene Christian College. Although successful as a music educator, he took a different direction on graduate degrees in view of the job market and available positions for music educators, particularly in higher education.

After completing his master of education degree in elementary education and special education at Sam Houston State University in Huntsville, Texas, in 1974, he taught high-school special education for a year and then fourth grade in Madisonville, Texas, for a year, preparing a diversified set of experiences for his eventual college audiences.

He completed his PhD in educational curriculum and instruction at Texas A&M in 1979. He returned to public-school teaching in the 1980s during turbulent economic times in higher education, teaching emotionally disturbed and learning-disabled secondary students in schools in Texas and Oklahoma. In the 1980s, he returned to graduate school to complete certification work in educational leadership. He has been certified for the principalship at elementary and secondary levels in both Oklahoma and Texas. Dr. Womack is now professor of secondary education at Arkansas Tech University, where he has been for the past twenty-three years. He is an elder in the church that he attends. He has written several refereed articles and made several refereed presentations on educational leadership. He is a board member for a children's home in Arkansas.

Introduction

What is it like to be a superintendent of a school district? At any given moment in time in the United States, about 14,000 people know from personal experience. Only about 14,000 people know—not the millions of teachers, support personnel, and lower-level administrators across our nation's 98,000 school campuses. This book is written especially to give a vision of the superintendency to hopefuls who would like to someday join those 14,000.

We wrote this book to try to be of help to those individuals. We particularly wanted to be of help with the feelings and sensations of a new superintendency. If one is looking for sage advice about how to manage and lead a large school district like a twenty-year veteran, he or she might consult tomes such as Theodore J. Kowaski's *The School Superintendent: Theory, Practice, and Cases,* 2nd ed. Our book is designed more to help the person who has had some experience as a building principal and feels that he or she is ready for the central-office experience. It attempts to answer the questions: What is the first year going to be like? and What are the first experiences going to be like?

We enlisted the help of two dozen current superintendents to help us create this book, organize the information, and put it into hopefully digestible language. We asked these superintendents, particularly those who had no more than three or four years of experience and who therefore would have had less opportunity to forget those first-year experiences, to answer a questionnaire. Some of our respondents had been CEOs of school districts longer than three or four years, and we included their responses; but we tried to especially highlight those from the new superintendents.

There is a tendency on the part of most people to look back at situations with a mental eraser. We tend to mentally suppress the mistakes and remember the victories. That is why we relied especially upon the ethnographic data given us by the newest superintendents. This book was written especially to those who may be going into such positions within the next year or two. It is designed to answer the question: What will the first year feel like?

After much deliberation, we settled on these questions for our questionnaire:

1. How did you move into your new superintendent's office? Alone or with family or friends to help? Which items did you put within an arm's reach and which ones did you put furthest away in a file cabinet or other place? Now, a year later, would you make changes to the way you moved into the office for the first time?

2. What kind of people came to see you early in your superintendency? How sincere were they? Did they seem to have students' interest as a first priority or did they have some other kind of agenda? How well did you feel you handled those "visits"? Did your visitors offer support or bring threats if they did not get their way?

3. When you delved into the accounting of your new school district, what kinds of surprises did you find? Were there things that you found that really made you worried that you might not be able to pull the district out of its undiscovered mess? What kinds of hidden plusses did you find?

4. What did you bring to your board on that first meeting? How ambitious would you say the first agenda was? Did the board in its first meeting with you ask for anything that really "stretched" you—that seemed like it would be difficult to deliver?

5. What kinds of things did you do in your first meeting with your central office staff and/or principals and supervisors? Did they seem intimidated by your expectations? In hindsight, the administrators that seemed most friendly and supportive—did they turn out to really be that way over the next year or two?

6. What was the first encounter with an angry parent or patron like? Had the parent gone through the chain of command before coming to you? Did the parent or patron seem to be playing craftily with you to try to get you to make a classic upper-management mistake? Describe this.

7. Renting/leasing school property and buying property: How successful were you in keeping your district out of the proprietary role in sharing facilities with the community?

8. Running a bond election: How successful were you in getting it to pass? How did you do that?

9. First significant legal challenge: How effective was your legal counsel in working with you and your board? How did you know that a situation that was brought to you was one that would need legal advice?

10. Your first evaluation of supervisory staff: How accepting were your principals, etc., of your first evaluation? If they questioned the validity of your evaluation, what kinds of things did they contest? On what kinds of things did they say, "Yes, this was absolutely right, and I will go to work on improving this area of my leadership"?

11. What kind of trend in academic achievement did you see your first year? To what extent did those trends reflect your leadership, as compared to a carry-over from the previous superintendent? After the first year, did you change some programs, approaches, methods, curricula, etc.? Describe what you did and the acceptance by staff, effects, etc.

We could have asked other questions, but we wanted to center upon the issues that soon-to-be central-office administrators would most want to know. Knowing the demands upon superintendents' time, we also wanted to keep the list of questions brief enough for them to want to answer the questions instead of filing the questionnaire in the trash can. We made a spreadsheet to help us sift and sort through the data. In qualitative ways, we sought to find out which issues the more experienced administrators focused on, as compared to the relative newcomers to the central office. We are grateful for their responses and the rich answers they gave, which often more than fully answered our questions.

We spent some time on the issue of whether to write everything in third person (trying to sound more objective and academic) or let at least some parts of it be in second person. All three of us have published and presented before. We as a team did not write the book so much to demonstrate our scholarship as to help new superintendents settle into their positions with as little extraneous stress and distraction as possible.

There will be some variance in the person of the book, including "you" passages written to you as soon-to-be superintendents. We do so without apologies. In places, our experienced superintendent, Dr. Roberts, adds his experiences to what our survey and the professional literature have to say. We hope you find our book both professionally beneficial and personable.

Kerry L. Roberts
Sid T. Womack
Shellie Lyne Hanna

Chapter One

What Kinds of People Become Superintendents?

The school superintendent is hired by the school board as the educational leader of the school district. Superintendents are the chief executive officers. Their sole purpose is to make certain that the district is run efficiently and effectively so all students can learn. They direct all aspects of the school, from curriculum to management to facilities.

According to Glass, Bjork, and Brunner (2000), citizens think the superintendent is the expert on all educational matters in the community. The school board thinks and believes the superintendent is the "swami" of all educational wisdom. Glass and colleagues do acknowledge that the role of the superintendent is politically charged, more so than ever before.

That is why Cunningham and Burdick (1999) conclude that many highly qualified people will not move to the superintendent position because of the job it has become. Therefore, it is imperative that one understand the value of educating them about what the current trends in education curriculum are, as well as issues of importance to community members.

The administrator who desires to become a superintendent is an educator who wants to have an impact on student achievement and enjoys working toward that goal. When he or she finally aspired to the goal of becoming a school superintendent and signed that first contract, there was silent jubilation and then a realization of "what have I gotten myself into?"

Superintendents are competitive by nature and don't mind the challenges they will be facing. That is why the majority of superintendents come from coaching and music backgrounds. Therefore, they don't tend to dwell long on the negative, but quickly start looking for ways to improve the education within the school district, so the students who graduate will be contributors to the town and society.

These new superintendents have spent the past year sending out many job applications and resumes to districts that were looking to hire a superintendent. Sometimes they sent out their professional materials to districts they really weren't interested in because the market is a soft market and they strongly wanted a superintendent position. Upon receiving notice of being the lone finalist, the candidate's heart " leaped for joy" because of the knowledge that he or she was going to be the next superintendent in that district. That process is tedious and onerous, but for this rare breed of educators it is well worth it.

The personalities who have moved into superintendents' offices have been characterized in many ways; many articles and books have been written about them. Example 1.1 shows what the Interstate School Leadership Licensure Consortium conceptualizes for district leaders.

Example 1: Interstate School Leadership Licensure Consortium Standards for All School Administrators (Kowalski, 2006, p. 23)

Standard

1. A school administrator is an educational leader who promotes the success of all students by facilitating the development, articulation, implementation, and stewardship of a vision of learning that is shared and supported by the school community.
2. A school administrator is an educational leader who promotes the success of all students by advocating, nurturing, and sustaining a school culture and instructional program conducive to student learning and staff professional growth.
3. A school administrator is an education leader who promotes the success of all students by ensuring management of the organization, operations, and resources for a safe, efficient, and effective learning environment.
4. A school administrator is an educational leader who promotes the success of all students by collaborating with families and community members, responding to diverse community interests and needs, and mobilizing community resources.
5. A school administrator is an educational leader who promotes the success of all students by acting with integrity, fairness, and in an ethical manner.
6. A school administrator is an educational leader who promotes the success of all students by understanding, responding to, and influencing the larger political, social, economic, legal, and cultural context.

Say what you like, these are the core standards for central-office administrators in the United States. Goals and objectives for superintendent-prep graduate programs are written from the six statements in example 1.1.

The superintendent is the CEO of a district. What does the superintendent do? Conran (1989) describes a superintendent as the instructional leader. He also says the superintendent is the curriculum director, master teacher of principals, public-relations expert, and reporter.

Superintendents take on the roles of construction supervisor or rental agent, mediator of disputes, legal clerk, and investment counselor. They are purchasing agents and bookkeepers, strategic planners, guidance counselors, public speakers, lobbyists, negotiators, personnel supervisors, and oftentimes hosts (Conran 1989).

The superintendent has many duties and wears many hats. Building an educational system that allows students to learn to their fullest potentials and fits the superintendent's style will be the major priorities.

Success for the superintendent will be determined by how well that district leader shares with others, communicates, and builds relationships. Credibility will be determined by honesty and integrity, knowledge of the education system (putting research into practice), and decision-making abilities (fairness and competence). Managerial skills will be determined by the ability to utilize resources to their fullest potential (getting the most out of the taxpayers' dollars) and employee relations. In essence, these skills can be called the four *h*'s of leadership: hustle, heart, humor, and humility.

HUSTLE, HEART, HUMOR, HUMILITY

According to Merriam-Webster's Collegiate Dictionary (10th ed., 2001), **hustle** is defined by a means you have to move or act energetically; to act or sell aggressively, especially in business dealings. Hustle is, in essence, hard work. Hustle includes promptness, efficiency, and professionalism. It doesn't take talent to have hustle, but rather determination and attitude.

An unknown author said, "Play like you're in first, but train like you're in second." What makes a person or a business successful? It keeps coming back to the same word: *hustle*. It doesn't mean that you're working some kind of racket or scam. Hustle is akin to the professional athlete's credo of "playing with pain." The professional tennis player or football player performs at times when playing does not feeling good. The professional singer sings to some audiences when there is no music in her soul. That's hustle.

A good definition of what is meant by *hustle* includes the following:

1. Hustle is doing something that everyone is absolutely certain can't be done.
2. Hustle is getting commitment because you got there first, or stayed with it after everyone else gave up.
3. Hustle is shoe leather and elbow grease and sweat and missing lunch.
4. Hustle is getting people to say "yes" after they've said "no" twenty times.
5. Hustle is doing more for a customer than the other guy can do for him.
6. Hustle is believing in yourself and the business you're in.

Quality superintendents need that energy to get the right things done and the determination to see it through. "Things may come to those who wait, but only what's left behind by those that hustle," said Abraham Lincoln.

Heart is both courage and empathy. It takes *courage* and *heart* to go against the grain. In today's world, courage is a long-lost art. *Courage* comes from the Old French word *corage*, which means "heart and spirit." When you speak and lead from your heart and spirit, you are being true to yourself. Bud Wilkins (2001) echoed this when he said, "You can motivate players better with kind words than you can with a whip."

Quotes on Courage (2010) quotes the following authors as saying the following things:

- Charles Swindoll said, "Courage is not limited to the battlefield or the Indianapolis 500 or bravely catching a thief in your house. The real tests of courage are much quieter. They are the inner tests, like remaining faithful when nobody's looking, like enduring pain when the room is empty, like standing alone when you're misunderstood."
- Joshua understood courage when he entreated the Israelites by saying, "Only be you strong, and very courageous, then you will make your way prosperous, and then you will have good success." (Joshua 1:78)
- Gerald R. Ford said, "In the age-old contest between popularity and principle, only those willing to lose for their convictions are deserving of posterity's approval."
- John Wayne summed it all up, in a western way, by saying, "Courage is being scared to death, but saddling up anyway."

Students, teachers, principals, and boards hope for courage from their superintendents' but courage that knows when to act. *Courage* is different from brashness. Courage knows not only *how* to act but also *when* to act.

Cheryl Stone (2009), in her review of Margaret Morford's book *Management Courage: Having the Heart of a Lion*, lists six principles. These are the following:

1. Be painfully honest
2. Never treat people identically
3. Don't use individuals or policies as a crutch
4. Ask for and give real feedback
5. Take the blame
6. Leave soul-sucking situations.

Empathy is the ability to know our feelings and accurately sense the feelings of those around us. In essence, empathy is the ability to see with the eyes of another, to hear with the ears of another, and to feel with the heart of another (Fiore, 2004). Robert Tizon said, "I would rather have eyes that cannot see; ears that cannot hear, lips that cannot speak than a heart that cannot love." Kahlil Gibran (Khurana) said, "Tenderness and kindness are not signs of weakness and despair, but manifestations of strength and resolution." Bonnie Jean Wasmund said, "People will forget what you said, people will forget what you did, but people will never forget how you made them feel." (Wasmund)

Empathy follows the Golden Rule, "Do unto others as you would have them do unto you." This part of heart, in essence, is servant leadership. Alan Loy McGinnis said, "There is no more noble occupation in the world than to assist another human being to help someone succeed."

Spears (2010) lists the ten characteristics of the servant leader, which are listed in example 1.2. The second point he mentions is empathy.

Example 1.2 Ten Characteristics of a Servant Leader

1. Listening receptively
2. Acceptance of (and empathy with) others
3. Foresight and intuition
4. Awareness and perception
5. Highly-developed powers of persuasion
6. Ability to conceptualize and communicate concepts
7. A healing influence upon people and institutions
8. Ability to build a sense of community in the workplace
9. Practice contemplation
10. Willingness to change

According to Sultanoff (1995), **Humor** is wit, mirth, and laughter. To define these three components of humor, Sultanoff (1995) defines them as: "Wit is the cognitive experience, mirth the emotional experience, and laughter the physiological experience." (p.1). Humor is very important to business health. It has the same qualities to business as it has to mental health. Humor helps us relate to others and be part of the group. Humor reduces stress and an example of this was when my father was being "chewed out" by his supervisor, while he was eating his lunch. He said, when he was finished eating the chicken leg, "when you're finished chewing on me, you can now chew on this bone." The supervisor started laughing and the humor helped stop the tension. Humor takes the stress and helps them see a different world from a different perspective. It takes distressing emotions and replaces them with elating feelings. Humor, as in the example, changes how we behave and deal with others and it decreases hormones caused by stress. Finally humor helps increase our energy and make up more productive and, for good measure, it makes us feel good. It is a good medicine for our heart (Sultanoff, 1995).

Researchers have linked humor to leadership and the ability to effect change in followers (Avolio et al. 1999). *The Encyclopedia of Leadership* states that leadership humor is significant yet complex. Humor can be highly positive and enhance dialogue yet may cause resistance or offer an opportunity to express pent-up resentment. Therefore, while humor may generate stability and a sense of belonging, it can have disruptive effects (Collision 2004).

King Solomon, often considered the wisest man in the world, understood the importance of humor when he wrote in Proverbs 17:22 (KJV), "A merry heart doeth good like a medicine," and in Proverbs 15:13, "A merry heart maketh a cheerful countenance."

Vecchio, Justin, and Pearce (2009) found that low humor is associated with lower performance. Avolio and colleagues (1999) recommend that organizations consider using contingent rewards, honesty, integrity, and humor. They further conclude that the use of humor opens communications between leaders and followers and thereby enhances performance. President Dwight Eisenhower said, "A sense of humor is part of the art of leadership, of getting along with people, of getting things done." Reverend Billy Graham said, "A keen sense of humor helps us to overlook the unbecoming, understand the unconventional, tolerate the unpleasant, overcome the unexpected, and outlast the unbearable."

Vecchio, Justin, and Pearce (2009) conclude that the impact of humor in an educational setting may depend on "the leader's degree of integrity and the value that the follower places on the leader's use of contingent reward" (189). Miller (2008) found that a very important part of humor in the workplace is its relaxant effect. Humor eases stress, which affects both job satisfaction and job performance (Roberts 1983; James & Tetrick 1986; Mathieu & Zajac 1990).

Miller (2008) concludes from review of the Gunning (2001) study that "humor is important across all hierarchical levels" (17). She goes on to say that humor helps get the work done, relieves stress, and helps maintain objectivity and rationality. Humor, according to Gunning's findings, also helps create high morale, teamwork, and flexibility to new ideas. Miller does say that humor can be one-sided, and workers might not feel comfortable using humor with the supervisor.

Miller (2008), analyzing Susa's (2002) study, reports that Susa found that managers can increase employee performance with the use of relief humor. When supervisors use relief humor, they are perceived as being better problem solvers. Also, there is greater job satisfaction, commitment, creativity, attendance, and job performance.

In the Mawhinney (2008) study, it was concluded that humor increased social support amongs teachers and alleviated stress, while aiding in problem solving. Miller (2008) summarizes by saying that people using humor in positive ways enjoy positive results.

In reflection, humor is useful in communication in tenuous situations, in relieving stress, and in clarifying difficult topics in work groups. "Humor can be used to convey information, break down behavioral barriers, highlight key points, and identify where tension exists" (1). Supervisors can use humor in corrective situations without being threatening. Also,

> humor can also be used as a non-threatening way for subordinates to push back up the chain of command without overstepping customary lines of authority. Humor allows you to discuss taboo topics, including expression of certain emotions, such as aggression, fear, and sadness. Humor allows you to maintain lines of communication in spite of conflict. Humor's ability to facilitate communication is likely one of its most powerful and potentially useful aspects. (1)

Humility is the fourth *h* of leadership. It is an attribute that is often overlooked when we speak about leadership. Baldoni (2009) summarizes by saying that humility is essential to leadership, as it authenticates our humanity. He goes on to say that if you want to be an effective leader, you need to be humble. Lawrence (2010) defines humility as "down to earth, patient, compassionate, concerned, and authentic in sincerity," concluding that leaders with humility "act with modesty and restraint" (124).

A humble person is interested in others and in touch with reality, which includes strengths and limitations (Comte-Sponville, 2001). Lawrence (2001) says that the practices of exemplary leadership are modeling, inspiring, challenging, enabling, encouraging, and acknowledging are only possible if one has authentic humility. According to Bose (2010), a leader has qualities that will raise him or her above the rest. Every individual around the leader will be aware of this. However, humility is the attribute that makes a good leader more approachable.

Approachability allows for better communication between a leader and a team, therefore allowing a leader to know of the problems that the team is facing. Bose also says that approachability and humility place a leader in a position where team members provide suggestions that may be valuable. In summary, being humble is an important characteristic of an effective leader.

A sense of humility is essential to effective leadership because it validates a person's humanity. Leaders who want to inspire followership need to demonstrate not only their accomplishments but their character. Hoekstra and colleagues (2008) say that "humility in leadership is back on the executive conference room table. It should have never left the table. But fortunately . . . both leadership scholars and practitioners alike have re-discovered its importance" (79).

Finally, another major characteristic of the superintendency is *isolation*. The individual needs to be aware of this to prepare for the loneliness of the position. Isolation has been documented as "coming with the territory" at all levels of administration, including the principalship, as well as the superintendency (Kippeny 1989; Jones 1994; Parish 2001, 2002; Crosby 2004; Ullrich 2006; Houston 2008; Gifford 2009).

Wheeler H. Robinson said, "The penalty of leadership is loneliness." Leadership is a lonely world . . . because you gain members, who indeed believe in your ideology and leadership skills, and you lose the so-called friends, and not only them, but those you had trust and belief in them. It's lonely at the top.

As one grief-stricken administrator confided when her husband died, "Dr. Roberts, it's so lonely at the top." Myers (2009) says, "Privileges and handlers surround leaders, giving them little access to new ideas. They would gain from an open forum of diverse people, listening more than speaking, and exposure to innovative ideas." Wajnert (2010) says,

> In some TV game shows, contestants are provided with lifelines to use if stress, indecision, unfamiliar circumstances or outside pressures inhibit their ability to answer questions correctly or perform well. Unfortunately, CEOs today are often metaphorically at sea, at risk, and without a lifeline.
> In the past few years, the failure rate of CEOs has increased significantly even as average tenure has dropped sharply. Performance issues, incompatibility with increasingly active boards of directors, worldwide recession pressures, government intervention and shareowner activism have combined to threaten the future of longstanding and previously successful executives. The resulting turnover has placed CEOs in difficult environments without much support.

Jorgenson and Peal (2008) say that "many teachers believe that their administrators have lost touch with life in the classroom, and the resulting gap is a serious concern. Closing a perception gap between principals and teachers is critical if they are to work together for their mutual benefit and that of the children they serve." Even the teachers themselves feel that they teach in isolation (Kassissieh & Barton 2009).

Geographic isolation can exacerbate feelings of social isolation (Duncan & Stock 2010). If the superintendent as an individual is physically separated in another building or area of the city, the isolation is greater because the perception of social isolation will increase. It is important for the superintendent to be out in the schools and around the teachers and administrators frequently. Mentoring can also be a means of reducing the isolation felt by principals and increasing the connectedness of new teachers to their principals (Robinson, Horan, & Nanavati 2009). Through mentoring, teachers, principals, and superintendents are able to build relationships. Mentoring also gives a professional another adult person to work with *directly* toward common goals, thus lessening the isolation.

Beyond isolation, the person who wants to become a superintendent needs to understand that willingness to move around may be a necessity of the job. Good (2008) says that in his analysis of studies over 30 years, the average tenure of a superintendent ranged from 5.7 to 7 years. A 2008 study conducted by the Council of Greater City Schools found that the average number of years for the 53 urban superintendents interviewed was 3.5 in each district. They also state that in many smaller districts in rural areas, length of employment is longer.

Waters and Marzano (2006) found that as length of tenure went up, student achievement went up, at a level of .19 with significance at .05. School boards, however, do not always look at statistics and research when determining whether or not to keep a superintendent. Often personal agendas, personality issues, and so on may cloud the issue of how long someone should stay under contract with the district.

Superintendents display items that have significance to them on their walls and on their shelves. Pictures demonstrate their character or faith. One superintendent who loved to play golf and was highly religious put on his wall a picture of a golf hole with a scripture verse under it. He also had a picture of an executive sitting dejectedly in his chair, and Jesus was standing by him. Finally, he had two laminated sayings; one was about attitude and the other about Jesus. His father was a railroader, and, to show his roots, he had a couple of pictures of depots. On his shelf he had a train engine and golf trinkets. Finally, his shelf contained pictures of his wife and his children.

Another superintendent had his first report card framed. He had it on his wall with other articles about himself and his accomplishments. He also had many plaques. All of the superintendents had the numerous plaques they had received for various reasons.

Following is a checklist that will assist you as you assume the role of a superintendent of schools. The individual wanting to become a superintendent needs to be one that employs these types of activities, practices, and personality traits.

CHECKLIST

Building Educational System
__ Developing and amending policies.
__ Maintaining and exceeding educational excellence.
__ Improving curriculum and instruction.

Developing Relationships
__ Communicating for results (desired publics and stakeholders).
__ Having quality board-agenda packets that are easy to navigate.
__ Developing and maintain positive public relations.
__ Using networking.
__ Using mentoring.
__ Using sponsoring.
__ Reporting (required and voluntary).

Developing Credibility
__ Advocating research-based practice.
__ Using decision-making models for quality decisions.
__ Determining trends and implications.
__ Planning for growth, decline, and changing demographics.
__ Utilizing strategic and other planning models.
__ Telling the truth and not "spinning."

Managerial Skills
__ Utilizing conservative budgeting skills.
__ Getting the most for the taxpayer dollar.
__ Working with professionals (architect, attorney, investment banker, etc.).
__ Keeping buildings and grounds appealing.
__ Maintaining safe grounds and inspections.
__ Utilizing integrity and compassion in human relations (hiring, firing, retaining, contract negotiations).

SUMMARY

Teachers who become superintendents usually care very strongly for students and their achievement. They want to be able to make a positive difference in the student's life. The *Herald News* has reported that 48.5 percent of future superintendents move from being a teacher, to assistant principal or principal, to central-office administrator before taking their first position as superintendent.

Areas in education that tend to provide a lot of the superintendents are coaching and music. To acquire a superintendent's license, applicants must demonstrate that they meet that state's standards by taking a test that is meshed with the Interstate School Leaders Licensure Consortium (ISLIC) standards. The superintendent is the CEO of the district and, to be successful, should possess the four *h*'s of leadership: hustle, heart, humor, and humility. The four *h*'s of leadership are embedded in servant leadership.

Because of the position of the superintendency, it is a lonely position. The person who seeks this position must get his or her satisfaction from helping students succeed because, as the adage goes, *it's lonely at the top.*

REFLECTION QUESTIONS

1. Why did I decide to become a superintendent?
2. What are my character traits from the lists that are strengths?
3. Which character traits do I need to work on improving?
4. What will I do to lessen the perception that I have lost touch with the classroom?
5. Can I? Or how will I handle isolation?
6. Using the checklist provided, determine your readiness to become a superintendent.

Chapter Two

What Was "Moving In" Day Like?

How did you move into your new superintendent's office? Alone or with family or friends to help? Which items did you put within an arm's reach and which ones did you put furthest away in a file cabinet or other place? Now, a year a later, would you make changes to the way you moved into the office for the first time?

For someone who has built his or her life's work toward becoming a superintendent, moving into a superintendent's office for the first time is a grand event. It's more than graduation day. It's more than just getting the license. Moving in is a real "coming of age" event, a defining moment.

From the responses of the twenty-four superintendents in our study, most superintendents tend to move in by themselves. There is usually someone to help a superintendent move in. This has to do with the physical act of lifting boxes. When the boxes are in the room, the superintendents set up their items as they like. Following are recollections of some of the respondents.

A superintendent in Western Arkansas wrote,

My husband helped me move into my new office. He carried boxes and I put everything in its place. I put family pictures, my "happy wagon folder," plants, teaching license and doctoral diploma at my fingertips. I did not bring anything with me other than my personal professional development documentation that I filed in a file cabinet. I would not do anything differently if I were to move in a year later.

A superintendent in East Texas said,

I began by moving myself into the new office. My wife was still at our old house. Each week during the twenty-one-day waiting period, I would bring a few boxes from my old office. During the summer after school was out, my wife then helped to bring the rest of my office materials and decorations. On my desk I have a Rolodex, in-box, laptop, and phone. Just behind my desk on shelves I have a folder organizer that contains documents that I frequently need to reference. Now that I have been here a year, I would not make any changes. The setup I have now is what I used as a HS principal and it proved to be effective for me.

Another superintendent said that the items that he moved closest to his desk were his Bible, notebook, laptop, and phone, and a picture of his family. Farthest away from his desk were his diplomas, awards, and a clock. Looking back at it later, he would not change a thing.

A superintendent in a large Arkansas district who was reflecting on his first superintendency said of his moving-in day, "I moved in by myself. My files are within arm's reach and a few key books. My wife rearranged my bookshelf when she came to town . . . I would probably leave it all the same."

One superintendent wrote in considerable detail about his first moving-in experience. He said,

I can remember when I moved into the office. No one helped me move in. I parked the car and started to unload my materials for my office. This included books, certificates, diplomas, pictures, file folders, and some office knick-knacks. District personnel are watching you as you move in but are probably afraid to approach the new superintendent. So you make several trips by yourself. When you get into the office you set it up in a manner that would be comfortable to you. You want your office to be comfortable as physical atmosphere means a lot to your attitude towards the job.

The superintendent's secretary, who had been there for over thirty years and who was described by one board member to me as the "queen bee" of the district, did show me what was kept in each file. If I needed any history about the district, I just needed to talk to her. I later found out that she could "make you or break you."

When I started to set up the office, I kept a three-ringed binder of sample letters at my fingertips. I also kept a book about the superintendency, the state school rule book, the state directory, telephone book, policy manual, and a few other helpful books at my fingertips. Files that I kept in close proximity were those of a personal measure (i.e. license, resume, transcripts, letters of recommendation, references, etc.). Close to that file I kept a list of the board members with their pertinent information. I put reference books and files, that I felt were not of immediate importance, on the bookshelf or in a lower file drawer.

Throughout the year some items moved over to the shelf and lower-file drawer and others were put in the file on my desk. Those items that made it to my desk, and should have been there sooner, were the Negotiated Agreement, budget items, and board packets (one year). Items that flowed back and forth were items such as bond issues, building projects, and so forth. One item that should have come to my desk and stayed there was the *strategic plan.* At this point, I did not realize the importance of it.

One thing I discovered is that you need to have a good filing system. Since so many papers come across your desk, you need to know what is worth filing, what is for action, what is for immediate action, and what is for the wastepaper basket. You are the leader of the district and it's your job to keep the board informed, not when things happen, but before things happen.

A superintendent in Kansas had a different move-in experience. He had already worked in the district office and was promoted from deputy superintendent to superintendent. He described his experience as follows:

I took my time moving into my office. The former superintendent left at the end of May and the new deputy superintendent was not going to be in the office until late June. Therefore, I had about a month to slowly move things from one office to the new office (I was in the same building—serving as the deputy superintendent previously). The basics such as my computer and desk items were the first to get moved. I then took a lot of time combing through files that were left in the superintendent's office before bringing over files from my old office. I still have a few items left in my old office, but for the most part, everything is now in my new office. Access to email and internet and my documents on my computer are the majority of what I must have access to. That is one huge benefit to the technology that is currently at our fingertips.

Items that superintendents in our study tended to put "within arm's reach" (called *tier I*) were the policy manual, teacher's negotiated agreement, state rules and regulations, telephone books (city and district), and state education directory, as well as a few select professional books. One of these books was the *School Superintendent's Complete Handbook*. Other select books would be a favorite book about school finance, school law, facilities, curriculum, personnel, or school-administration research, and several superintendents had the Bible or a book of faith. A jump drive (technology) was mentioned as being on tier I, as Mr. H— said he had all his years of work on it.

From this tier I of books, you could move to a tier II of books. These are books that the superintendent felt were very important but did not move to the top tier. He or she usually had these on a bookshelf to the side of the desk. It was interesting to see what books they had selected. A few superintendents did not like to display any book, as they felt it made their offices look too cluttered, so they had their books in a shelving unit with doors.

Tier III books, those that are there in case you need them, were kept in cabinets out of the way. One superintendent had his compliance manuals in tier III because he did not need to look at those as often. Many of these books needed to be culled, but the superintendent did not want to part with them for some reason or other.

One respondent said, "When I moved in, family and friends helped me. Those items I keep closest to me are my jump drive which contains years of work and I use it every day. The items furthest from me are my compliance manuals. They would be on my shelves [tier III]. I would renovate the office before I moved in instead of after."

Looking at the past and reflecting if they would set up their offices differently, all of the respondents in the study said they would do it the same way again. That says that once a pattern of organization in the office is set, it should be continued because it is comfortable. The superintendents could not see any reason for changing things unless it made their job more efficient and helped them do their job better. One superintendent did say that he would not move in as many items as he did, because if he ever had to move it would take him longer to move out.

The physical office of the superintendent tells the person coming into the office who the superintendent is and his or her likes and dislikes, passions, and character. An office is a reflection of the person who works in it. Crager (2009) says the office should be warm and inviting. Guests need to feel welcome, and you need to be feel excited about the work emanating from that office.

The office should be a place where work can be optimized. Surround yourself with items that invigorate you and allow you to be creative. Office furniture should be professional and useful. The office should be arranged in a way that makes work inviting. Quito (2009) found in her research that most people felt that art was important to the organization and its identity, but it was irrelevant to worker performance and the company mission. She also found that when there is "ambivalence to the art, it can result in art demoted to decoration, alienation of audience, staff dissent, and missed opportunities for learning." Her thesis argues that art is a tool that makes the organization's vision and values come to life. In other words, this is what we are and what we are all about. Choose artwork carefully because it speaks volumes about the person in the office.

Most superintendents kept the office as it was and only started to redecorate, rearrange, and so forth as they became more acquainted with the "lay of the land." One superintendent did get new furniture as the furniture that was there was old and "should have been in a museum." He wanted to portray to the public that the district cared for all aspects of education, especially student learning. The superintendents did repaint their offices and lay new carpet.

The majority of superintendents kept the furniture that was in the office. This is due to the fact that wise executives do not want to portray to the public that they are spending taxpayer money on the central office instead of the students. Roberts, in an unpublished paper (1980), reported on a study he'd conducted about how the physical building can stress students and teachers. The review of the literature found that colors, shapes, layout, and lighting played a big role in morale and the "inviting" aspect of the school, which was associated with student learning. Vischer (2007) came to the same conclusions from her research.

A checklist has been developed for you to use as you set up your office.

CHECKLIST

Tier I
__ Select professional books.
__ State rules and regulations.
__ School law book.
__ Dictionary.
__ Telephone books (city and district).
__ State department of education telephone book.
__ Faith book or Bible.
__ Jump drive.
Tier II
__ Professional books (books from administration classes).
__ Professional-organization books (i.e., AASA, ASCD, NSBA, etc.).
__ Books for professional development.
__ Handbooks on research (curriculum, administration, communications, etc.).
__ Guidebooks.
Tier III
__ Books that are outdated but that might be of some help.
__ Statistics books and APA books.
__ State compliance manuals.
__ Other books.
__ Three-ringed binders.
Wall
__ Diplomas (college).
__ Certificates or licenses.
__ Calendar.
__ Clock.
__ Pictures/art of value to us.
__ Framed report card or newspaper article.
__ Awards or plaques.
Pictures
__ Wife or husband.
__ Children.

__ Grandchildren.
__ Family pet.
Mementos
__ Items that tell people who you are (e.g., golfing paraphernalia, toy locomotive, trumpet).
__ Keep this sparse so it doesn't look to busy or cluttery. (Remember, you have to dust it.)

SUMMARY

When the superintendent moves in, it's usually only the superintendent who does the moving; if anyone helps him, it's his or her spouse. Several superintendents gave their responses as to how they moved into the superintendent's office and said they would do it the same way again if and when they took another position. The next chore after moving in was deciding where to put items and how to arrange the office.

REFLECTION QUESTIONS

1. What books would you put in Tier 1, Tier II, or Tier III? Why?
2. If you were hired as a superintendent and you were given a normal or 12X15 office with windows on one wall, how would you design the layout? Would you change the furniture? Would you repaint or re-carpet? Why?
3. How would you place your furniture? Does that make your office inviting or distant?
4. What is dear to you that you would put on your shelves and hang on your wall?

Chapter Three

What Kinds of People Visit the New Superintendent Right Away?

What kind of people came to see you early in your superintendency? How sincere were they? Did they seem to have students' interest as a first priority or did they have some other kind of agenda? How well did you feel you handled those "visits"? Did your visitors offer support or bring threats if they did not get their way?

When a person interviews for a superintendent's position, the board or head-hunter usually visits with all of the stakeholders, so they know what they are looking for. This is called "finding the right person." The list of qualities desired for this "perfect superintendent" is derived from all of these visits.

The stakeholders can include teachers, students, parents, administrators, school-board members, classified building staff members, counselors, community members, retired community members, business leaders, local (non-parent) business-community members, pastors, local public-service-agency members (police, fire, etc.), chamber-of-commerce members, local/state politicians, and so forth.

A committee is formed that has representation from all of these groups, so they can have input into defining what is desired from the next superintendent. The desired traits are generally ones that inspire trust and self-confidence, and that model high standards of integrity and personal performance, along with the ability to develop and communicate a vision of quality education for the future to the board, staff, and community. The checklist at the end of this chapter lists traits desired of superintendents.

When the new superintendent takes office, power brokers of the community, some shareholders, parents, teachers, administrators, and so forth will come and visit the new superintendent right away. Many of these people just

19

want to get a chance to meet the new superintendent, but some want the new superintendent to know their power roles in the community. A few parents will have gripes veiled as "concerns." Black and English (1986) conclude that good administrators feel at ease with people. They go on to say that they know how to deal with power positively, to develop unity, and to move people and with people to common goals. They "must be able to win people rather than force people" (10).

That is why first impressions are so important. The new superintendent will have power brokers and shareholders visiting, and the impression made on these people will spread like wildfire in the community. First impressions matter especially when you want to build a lasting trust. These will make or break the superintendent.

Thompson (2008) writes, "First impressions (what others think of a person at a glance) can tell us a lot about another person, and several psychological studies have shown they can predict success in areas such as running for elected office or teaching. But how well a teacher teaches and how much a candidate appeals to voters are both subjective ideas." He goes on to say that researchers Rule and Ambady of Tufts University found that first impressions could predict performance of a CEO.

Research by Bar, Neta, and Linz (2006) found that our first impressions can be truthful and are formed by using, "the visual appearance especially of the faces." Dye (2004) says, "If first impressions really do matter the most, then that first meeting ought to have a predictable impact, and the researchers say they found that to be the case" Dye (2004) goes on to write, "First impressions are the most important, according to new research showing that the opinions we form in the first few minutes after meeting someone play a major role in determining the course of the relationship." Coming across wrong to the wrong people can doom your tenure at the new school district. This all adds up to power, and "to have a winning hand you must have friends" (12). As the saying goes, "Enemies accumulate, friends don't."

An example of what school districts are looking for in a superintendent is found in a Ray and Associates brochure for the Derry Township School District (Derry, PA). The school district is seeking a superintendent who. . .

1. Is a strong communicator (speaking, listening, and writing);
2. Inspires trust, has high levels of self-confidence and optimism, and models high standards of integrity and personal performance;
3. Possesses excellent people skills and presents a positive image of the district but will listen to input and make a decision when necessary;
4. Has knowledge of and successful experience in sound fiscal practices and management of district resources, including appropriate participation of others in planning and decision-making;
5. Has demonstrated strong leadership skills in previous positions;

6. Is able to identify and select building and central office administrators who are capable of advancing the district's vision;
7. Is strongly committed to a *student first* philosophy in all decisions;
8. Is able to delegate authority appropriately while maintaining accountability;
9. Makes recommendations and decisions are data-driven; and is able to lead a large organization dedicated to goals of continuous improvement.

Another example is in the following advertisement by Hazard, Young, Attea, Associated, Ltd., another search firm, for the Beaverton School District (Beaverton, OR), which illustrates what is being sought after in a superintendent.

After consultation with Beaverton School District internal and external stakeholders, the Board of Education seeks a student-centered educator exemplifying the following characteristics:

A person of *high moral character* who possesses the following personal traits and characteristics:

- A good listener who makes others feel at ease and comfortable sharing their views and ideas.
- A life-long learner who is open to new ideas.
- A person of integrity, honesty, and genuineness capable of building trust and rapport with all constituents.
- Someone who demonstrates an unwavering commitment to fairness, a strong conviction for equity, and a deep respect for diversity and social justice.

A *visionary leader* who embodies the following leadership style:

- A systems approach to organizational improvement which defines the mission, vision, and goals of the organization and implements the District's strategic plan in order to achieve those goals.
- Collaborative strategies for decision-making, with decisiveness when the time is right and/or necessary.
- Great communication skills that seek input from stakeholders and keep everyone informed on both the "what" and the "why" regarding decisions being made.
- Team building approaches that value everyone's contribution to the organization and help individuals fulfill their roles in achieving of the goals of the organization.

A *committed educator* who possesses the following professional skills and knowledge sets:

- An understanding of the learning process that guides the organization in delivering outstanding instructional programs designed to support the individual growth of all learners, while respecting and supporting the professional knowledge, commitment, and abilities of the staff.
- Recognition that technology will play an integral role in educating students and an understanding of how to move the district forward in implementing technology to support student learning and district operations.
- Understanding of the financial issues facing the school district with a record of implementing strategies useful in addressing those challenges.
- Willingness and ability to serve as a statewide leader to help improve educational opportunities for all children and a commitment to be in Beaverton for the long term.
- An *earned doctorate* from a nationally recognized university or college and experience as a superintendent in a similar school district are highly desirable, but not required.

An East Texas superintendent said,

> Surprisingly, I had few visits. The visits I did receive include a Region Seven Field Service Agent, a TASB representative, and a few parents. None seemed to have an agenda other than wanting to be of help to me and answer any questions I may have. A few teachers stopped by to request things, which I now know was an attempt to get something that they were not able to get before. I feel I handled all visits well. As far as the teachers are concerned, my response to them was that I would be spending some time evaluating and would make those type decisions at a later date. None of the requests were pressing.

A superintendent in a small school district in Arkansas said of the first visits, "Especially when you were as young as I was my first year as a superintendent, you learn to listen a lot and say only a little. Almost anybody who shows up right away at your office has an agenda. Make almost no promises."

One superintendent said that his first visitors were board members, teachers, administrators, pastors, and youth directors. All seemed very sincere in what they were doing. He tried to listen to their concerns. Some had personal agendas, but all of his visitors stated that they wanted what was best for the students.

Another superintendent reported that "the first couple that visited our home, which is on campus, were two retired teachers that lived in the district. The curriculum coordinator visited my office and had a plant delivered from the staff. All of my visits were supportive and nobody seemed to have an 'agenda.'"

Another superintendent, one now of a large school district, said of his first superintendency's first visitors, "Most of the people who came to see me were 'city politicians' but they were sincere in just welcoming me to town. They were almost exclusively support conversations so they were easy ones to have."

Another superintendent said, "One of my first visitors was the transportation director. He was also the head of the support union. He said, 'So you're the new superintendent. You're a liar because all superintendents are liars.'" Then he walked out. The superintendent went on to say that he worked hard to change the transportation director's perception of superintendents, and by the end of the first semester he was the superintendent's biggest supporter. This change came about because of constant communication, being honest in all dealings, being truthful, and caring for the transportation director's well-being.

These very early meetings will set the tone of what the whole administration is going to be like in the coming months and years. This is why first impressions are so very important. How does a brand-new superintendent handle these first few encounters in ways that show good character and positive expectations? The new superintendent needs to make it a priority to remember names and make people feel at ease. The key communication strength of the new superintendent has to be listening.

Superintendents build trust by communicating and showing concern. The message is clear and direct and is coupled with compassion. Bias (1994) concludes in her review of research that successful superintendents are those who understand the political nature of the superintendency and look forward to serving the communities' constituencies. She goes on to say they are proactive in seeking the support of the power groups within the community.

One respondent said the following: "I had lots of different people stop in or write me an email congratulating me on my appointment to the new position. Several teachers, the former mayor, CO staff members and BOE members. I was encouraged by the folks that took time to welcome me to my new job."

The superintendents' comments demonstrate that stakeholders show up and want to visit with the new superintendent. One superintendent clearly remembers when a parent (also a teacher in the district) and her husband showed up and wanted the high-school basketball coach fired. You might have guessed it, but they were unhappy with their son's playing time. Shortly after they left, a high-ranking official from the largest and most influential business in town came in and wanted to make certain nothing happened to the basketball coach. Then the flood broke: the banker, the board vice president, the teacher's-union president, various administrators, a newspaper reporter, and a host of others came by that first day. All of the visitors were sincere, and for the most part they were very cordial.

The only potential problem involved complaints about the basketball coach. That problem was brewing before the new superintendent arrived. What added fuel to this fire was the fact that the board got involved in it. Some liked the coach and some did not. This superintendent felt this was a no-win situation, as the coach had only been in the district one year and had previously been a successful college coach. After one month on the job, the board nonrenewed the basketball coach and a search was started for a new coach. Even though there was division in the district, the superintendent felt that his willingness to listen, treat people cordially, and get to the facts helped him through this tough time. He had made a very good first impression on his visitors.

CHECKLIST OF DESIRED SUPERINTENDENT TRAITS

___ Demonstrated strong leadership skills in previous positions.

___ Possesses the leadership skills required to respond to the challenges presented by an ethnically and culturally diverse community.

___ Delegates authority appropriately while maintaining accountability.

___ Is committed to a "student first" philosophy in all decisions.

___ Demonstrates effective communication skills to include speaking, listening, and writing.

___ Demonstrates the ability to enhance student performance, especially in identifying and closing or narrowing the gaps in student achievement.

___ Builds consensus and commitment among individuals and groups, with emphasis on parental involvement.

___ Makes data-driven recommendations.

___ Creates inviting and nurturing school culture and climate.

___ Promotes a positive working and learning environment.

___ Listens to input, but can make a decision when necessary.

___ Optimizes communication internally and externally with parents, students, patrons.

___ Engages students in school and community.

___ Is fiscally responsible.

___ Holds all levels of the organization accountable for continuous improvement in instruction and assessment, leading to achievement for all students.

__ Creates a standards-based curriculum that is communicated, aligned, and flexible to adapt to challenge and relevancy.

__ Provides optimal space for learning.

__ Promotes the safety and wellness of students and staff.

__ Examines, recommends, and implements proved instructional delivery models.

__ Identifies, implements, and tracks comprehensive staff development that aligns with strategic objectives.

__ Attracts and retains highly qualified and effective teachers.

SUMMARY

When a person interviews for a superintendent's position, the board or head-hunter usually visits with all of the stakeholders so they know what they are looking for. This is called "finding the right person." The list of qualities desired for this "perfect superintendent" is derived from all of these visits. The stakeholders includes teachers, students, parents, administrators, school board members, classified building staff members, counselors, community members, retired community members, business leaders, local business member (non-parent), pastors, local public service agency member (police, fire, etc.), chamber of commerce members, local/state politicians, and so forth. First impressions are important as new superintendent will have power-brokers and shareholders visiting him/her, and the impression made on these people will be spread like wildfire in the community. First impressions matter especially when you want to build a lasting trust. It will make or break the superintendent.

REFLECTION QUESTIONS

1. What do you think people will think about you as a first impression?
2. Have you considered asking someone whom you have recently met and who will be honest with you what his or her first impression was when you met? If you have done this, what did you learn?

3. Do you know what issues were important to different populations (parents, teachers, businesses, etc.) in the previous administration, an awareness of which might help to prepare you for situations that may arise early in your tenure? If the answer is no, do you want to do a little research in this area?

4. Why is trust building so important to superintendents? What can you do to help people whom you first meet have confidence and trust in you?

Chapter Four

Discovery: The Real State of the Fiscal Union

When you delved into the accounting of your new school district, what kinds of surprises did you find? Were there things that you found that really made you worried that you might not be able to pull the district out of its undiscovered mess? What kinds of hidden plusses did you find?

It is important for the superintendent to understand what is happening globally and nationally in the area of finance. Economic events in foreign markets, the International Monetary Fund, and the U.S. Treasury ultimately affect financial decisions at the district level. Successful superintendents are students of current events and economics.

The public schools are financed by the tax dollar, so the superintendent has to be aware of what is happening in the world. One new superintendent in our study was not aware of what was happening or adept to reading "the winds of change." He pushed through his new budget for the upcoming school year on a 4-3 vote. These types of votes (split) are not healthy for a superintendent's longevity. The concern of the three board members who voted against the new budget was that it raised the tax rate for the local taxpayers.

To further complicate this, the district received a $1.8 million grant for its middle school because it had failed to make adequate yearly progress for several years. The state worked with the district to identify where this money would be spent. One board member had some grave concerns because the district was doing all of this spending, wondering who was going to fund the middle-school changes three years later. That new superintendent needed to understand the state of the nation's and state's economies and learn how to do more with less money.

A quick primer in school finance is needed for an understanding of how public schools are funded.

a. **Local Property Tax**. Property taxes are a major source of funding for your schools. The school district levies an *ad valorem* tax on local properties to fund neighborhood public schools.

b. **State Funds**. State funds are another major source of support for most public school districts. These funds come from a variety of sources including sales, gasoline, franchise, and, in many states, income taxes.

c. **Federal Funds**. Compared to state and local funds, very little support actually comes from the federal budget, but these funds help support programs like free and reduced-price lunches, technology, bilingual education, Title I, Stuart McKinney migrant students, and special education. Some districts that have federal lands within their borders receive what is called "874" money, which is spendable for any ethical purpose.

d. **Grants**. Compared to the other funds, these are usually short-term funds, which means they will expire in a few years. A district applies for these or, as with the district above, qualifies for a grant because of its failure to make adequate yearly progress. One superintendent in our study said, "I discovered that our district was paying for all new teachers to receive their ESL endorsement through Title I funds. The district was changing drastically in its demographics and we are already at 69 percent Hispanic. We did have a healthy budget from state monies and federal funds as we were a Title I district."

School districts spend money on staff, materials and supplies, utilities, and buildings/grounds. School personnel, state and federal policy makers, and the community each play a role in influencing how much money is raised for education and how school funds are used. Typically 70 to 80 percent of the district budget is encumbered for salaries before classes ever meet for the first time in the fall. In some states, a minimum percentage of the overall budget (such as 70 percent) is mandated for salaries by state law. The relationship between schools, parents, and community and state policy makers is key to ensuring that our tax dollars are used prudently and for student achievement.

- **School personnel** and the school board make major budget decisions.
- **Policymakers** make rules on school funding and appropriations that determine how much money is available for education and how it should be allocated to different programs.
- **Community members** (parents, businesses, contractors) have a key role in making sure our tax dollars are used to fund schools fairly.

The new superintendent will learn how to get the most for the schools' dollar. This is through several strategies. One is wise **investing**. Ideally all available funds will be earning maximum interest daily. An assertive cash-management plan can realize significant additional revenues for the district. Another way of getting the most for your district's money is through **purchasing.** Learn the purchase-order policies and procedures. Make certain they are up-to-date and followed exclusively. The superintendent will want to develop friendly and helping relationships with staff and with vendors. The purchasing process should be viewed as a service. In choosing between products and vendors, "apples to apples" comparisons will need to be made. Make certain the quote price is for the same item. Some boards will set a maximum amount for the superintendent to spend on any one item, in any single purchase order, or with any one particular vendor without express board approval. It is wise to stay within the purchasing amount specified by the board.

The third way is through quality and effective **bookkeeping.** To the greatest extent possible, new technology should be utilized in performing bookkeeping functions. Duplications of effort should be avoided. The new superintendent needs to get it done right the first time, developing a system of checks and balances that will avoid mistakes and detect embezzlement.

Finally, make certain legal requirements are fulfilled.

Finance is a tricky business, and if the superintendent is not astute in this area, he or she will be a short-term superintendent. In contemporary times, superintendents have to be fiscally conservative and make certain that all moneys spent reflect the school district's mission statement.

School districts are in competition for these scarce resources. Accountability is essential. Students must come first in all decisions. Student learning is the reason given for why monies are spent in a given area. If cuts have to be made, the cut is made in the area that least affects student learning. Here are some examples of what was happening in the world of school finance in Texas in 2010. These may be typical of what was happening in other states as well:

a. BISD wins $18 million ins school transformation grants
b. Gilmer ISD automates food prepay
c. CISD looks at "robbing Hood" possibility
d. Perry puts the budget into perspective
e. Small town school district pulls itself back to the top
f. Superintendents in S.A. cautious on federal funding
g. S-TISD trustees ask for money to build new school
h. Brenham board finalizing tax rate
i. Burton ISD may avoid change in tax rate
j. Tax ratification election approved
k. Houston ISD expects budget overruns up to $39 million

l. Ingram school board to vote on budget proposal
m. Terrell ISD budget includes some staff cuts
n. Weatherford ISD reviews compensation package
o. Rural schools "do more with less" (national news)

These are surprises both good and bad. The superintendent has to be a quick learner in school finance. There is no excuse for the superintendent not knowing what is going on. Until the new superintendent "gets up to speed" in school finance, he or she should be conservative and make phone calls to the right people and the right people only. These calls are to colleagues, other superintendents, and the state department of education (finance department).

As one superintendent told us, "I didn't know that I had the most incompetent Chief Financial Officer in the state." Another superintendent told us, "I resigned because I trusted my assistant superintendent of finance and thought he was paying to the state the money the district owed. The community was not pleased when it found out how much the district owed to the state. Needless to say, that assistant superintendent is no longer with the district but the damage has already been done."

Given the *Mills v. Board of Education of the District of Columbia*, 348 F. Supp. 866, case, there are some budgetary options that cannot be taken. The superintendent cannot lower the level of funding for special education while leaving the budgets of other school programs the same. If special education takes a 10 percent hit, all programs must take a 10 percent hit.

A school-district budget is an estimate. According to Norton and colleagues (1996), a budget is made up of three elements: (1) description of total program; (2) estimate of expenditures; and (3) estimate of revenues. The key player in the preparation of these elements is the superintendent, not the chief financial officer. Remember, the budget doesn't control anything; *people* control costs and understand the budget.

Surprises can be numerous when delving into the accounting of a new district. It is our recommendation that the first duty of all new superintendents be to have an independent audit of the district. This will protect the district as well as the new superintendent. If there is no audit and an irregularity is later found, then it becomes difficult to "pin the blame" on the past superintendent. The costs of audits vary, but expect around $5,000 in 2010 dollars.

One superintendent whom we interviewed took over a district that was in fiscal distress. He had been made aware of it when he came to the district but had no idea what that meant until he got there. He did three things during the year that demonstrated he was aware of the situation and working to solve the problem. First, he informed the state department of education of the district's financial situation. Second, he kept in close contact with the finance department at the state department of education. And third, he kept in close communication with the district auditor while developing an action plan.

What was the end result? Because of the very good first impressions the superintendent made, the open-door policy he started, and the communication with shareholders, the superintendent was able to make some tough decisions, but the district came out of fiscal distress. To solve this potential problem, the superintendent got all of the key players together on a committee and laid the facts out before them. These stakeholders were in shock but were extremely appreciative of the openness of the superintendent.

This relationship and team building had to take place before the tough decisions could be made. After several meetings with this stakeholder committee, meetings with the auditor, and meetings with the state finance personnel, the superintendent was able to make some tough decisions with support from very unlikely sources. To come out of fiscal distress, a school had to be closed, teachers had to be reduced in force ("riffed"), support staff had to be riffed, all salaries were frozen, and only essential supplies were approved. It was a hard time, but the next year the district was out of fiscal distress and some of the cuts could be returned.

A superintendent polled in our survey said, "Accounting was kept well, but people were unhappy with the business department because they felt the person in charge had too much control." His district was a property-poor district, and he worried about meeting the budget. He quickly learned that his new district was a growing district and that students equaled money.

Another superintendent we surveyed said:

> I didn't realize the district had so many loopholes, but I should have expected it because they were having to pay back to the state $2,000,000 for overpayment. The previous superintendent had cut back everything to a skeleton crew. He didn't even replace his secretary and this was in a district of 6,200 students. This later proved problematic as the former superintendent was doing all of the secretarial work and his work. Policies that had been passed over two years ago were not in the policy book. We had to hire the retired secretary for a year to go back through all records to bring the policy book and other files up to date.

Yet another superintendent we polled said:

> I was surprised to see how much federal funding our district receives. I was also surprised at the large operating fund balance (in excess of $1,000,000 for a district of 639 students). I did not find any "skeletons in the closet" financially. The prior superintendent had shared many financial details with me prior to me agreeing to accept the position. . . .

A surprise for me was when I came out to this district as the superintendent; I
didn't realize that our budget for traveling for extracurricular activities was so
high. I was astonished and tried to cut it back but then found that was impossible. Our closest game in our league was 80 miles and our furthest game was
250 miles. We have four over-the-road busses for these long trips. Our location, out in the middle of nowhere dictated this travel expense.

A new superintendent in Kansas received a big surprise when the teachers'
negotiating team and the administration negotiating team could not come to
an agreement; they had been negotiating since February. The board did try to
settle and agreed to the $400,000 the teachers were asking for the insurance
pool. The sticking point was that the district team asked that administrators
be added, as the insurance pool excluded administrators. The teachers came
back and asked for $1 million.

A federal mediator was requested to solve this dilemma. The board president, who was an attorney, was negotiating for the district. The surprise to
this superintendent was the unwillingness of the teachers to budge. As mentioned at the start of this chapter, superintendents have to be aware of the
financial trends in the nation and world. The same superintendent said, "We
have a budget director that takes care of the budget. I have spent more time
with him this summer than in the past. Learning all of the dos and don'ts of
the budget has been interesting. What dollars can be spent on instruction
(general) vs. furniture (capital outlay) for example, has been discussed."

According to Sovine (2009), in his review of the literature, first-year
superintendents feel overwhelmed and underprepared to competently address
the challenges of the budget. Chapman (1997) found that board members
understand that financial issues are neither "created by the new superintendent nor within their powers to correct immediately" (14).

Of those polled who responded regarding the fiscal state of their districts,
68 percent said either that there were cuts that needed to be made, that they
were headed for distress, that they were in distress, or that they were in crisis.
At least 45 percent of the superintendents polled said they moved into districts in deep, deep financial distress. One of them seemed intent on project-
ing an image of, and behaving like, a "hatchet woman" who was more
concerned about money than anything else. This leads to back to the suggestion at the beginning of the chapter that if an audit has not been recently
performed by an outside, independent source, a new superintendent should
invest the time, money, and effort into this endeavor to help have an idea of
what he or she is really getting into.

CHECKLIST FOR SCHOOL FINANCE

__ Which bank or banks the district uses.

__ The limit the board has set on the superintendent for individual purchases, purchases without bids, and purchases from any single vendor within a given time period.

__ The sources of federal funding.

__ Which federal funds cannot be commingled with state or local money.

__ The name and phone number of the county tax assessor-collector.

__ The percentage of delinquent taxpayers within the county.

__ About the large taxpaying individuals or units in the district that are in arrears in their taxes.

__ The district's millage rate for maintenance and operations (M & O) and for bonded indebtedness.

__ What new money the district is getting for the coming school year.

__ The day of the month that the state's money is deposited in the local bank.

__ The amount of money that is in the activity account(s).

__ Who is on the list of district-approved personnel allowed to withdraw money from the activity account(s).

__ The district policy for paying out of the activity account(s).

__ The district policy for collecting gate receipts at athletic, music, or drama events.

__ What provisions have been made for security.

__ The policy for authorization of travel-reimbursement requests for teachers, support staff, and administration.

__ The policy on bids.

__ The policy on making bid requests known to the public.

__ The teacher salary scale and percentage of district revenues paid to salaries.

__ The administrative salary scale.

__ The support salary scale.

__ The costs of benefits for employees—costs such as Social Security, retirement, health insurance or a portion of health insurance, etc.

__ The benefits provided for each class of employees.

__ The current district grants.

__ Which grants may be available to the district with large, one-time items.

__ Which grants are available to the district with experiments in conjunction with the state and federal government.

__ The implications of new state finance laws.

SUMMARY

The superintendent is hired by the board and is responsible for the financial health of the school district. Public schools are financed by the public's money, which is through taxes. Therefore, the superintendent has to be very prudent is spending these monies. The goal is that these monies be used for student education. The relationship between schools, parents, and community and state policy makers is essential to ensuring that our tax dollars are used wisely for student achievement.

The superintendent has to be aware of the financial trends in the state, the United States, and even the world. The superintendent also needs to know how to look for ways to procure money from other areas (e.g., grants, advertisement). Other ways to increase the schools' financial standing are through investing and effective purchasing policies. The school is funded through local property taxes, state funds, federal funds, and grants. Understanding this is very beneficial to the new superintendent. A helpful suggestion to all new superintendents is to do an independent audit of your district when you first start. This will let you know your district's fiscal health.

REFLECTION QUESTIONS

1. When was your school district last audited, and what were the findings? Why are audits essential?
2. What areas of the budget seem to have surpluses/shortfalls? What improvements can be made to the budget that will best help the district meet its mission statement?
3. Begin to research why those surpluses/shortfalls may be occurring before making a decision about how to handle them. Write these out and then share them with your administrative staff and board of education.
4. Have you started to think about how you can best handle changes that need to be made and still effectively meet the district's goals? Write down your ideas, and have an in-service with your administrative team and board of education to discuss your findings.
5. What is the current procedure in your district for developing the budget? What changes need to be made? Is it effective and efficient?
6. Does the budget demonstrate that students come first in all decisions? If not, what needs to be done to accomplish that?
7. How does the new (or current) state finance law affect your district?

Chapter Five

The First Board Meeting

What did you bring to your board on that first meeting? How ambitious would you say the first agenda was? Did the board in its first meeting with you ask for anything that really "stretched" you—that seemed like it would be difficult to deliver?

The first board meeting is where the superintendent needs to put his or her "best foot forward." *It is a defining moment.* The superintendent has to set the right stage and tone for the physical meeting itself. In chapter 1 we talked about first impressions, and that is also important here. The atmosphere should be conducive to education, displaying dignity, professionalism, friendliness, and openness. The impression made to the board and to the public in a formal setting will be watched and scrutinized.

Before we discuss the tone and setting of the meeting, it's necessary to discuss the preparation for the meeting. The superintendent is in charge of the preparation, but all other participants (e.g., assistant superintendents, directors, principals, citizens) also need to be prepared. The board also needs to be prepared for the meeting. Board members need to read the board packet.

In the experience of one former superintendent, not all board members read their packet. That really put a lot of extra pressure on that superintendent, as he had to be extra alert and attentive in discussing each agenda item, so that when the board began their discussions, they could talk intelligently about the topic and make an intelligent decision. When a board member is not prepared for the meeting, there can be more turmoil due to excessive audience participation or poor planning for the meeting. It gives the appearance that education is not important to you or the board.

Davidson (1987) states, "The first responsibility is to make sure that each board member does the necessary homework. They should be familiar with the background and administrative considerations for each item" (103). He goes on to say that staff members should be prepared and should not have to leave the room to get additional materials. Citizens who wish to speak should be prepared, and signed in as guest presenters under the section "public to be heard." In this beginning section of the meeting, most board policies limit the time for a patron to speak to five minutes. Some districts have limited it to three minutes.

The physical setting of the room is extremely important. This includes lighting, temperature, and the microphone setup. According to Davidson (1987), the physical setting contributes to the tone and tenor of the meeting. Board meetings are to be conducted in business fashion. Districts are not businesses in the capitalist sense, but they do have to operate under good business practices. It is in this atmosphere that the superintendent projects his image to the public as being a good leader. Certificates, pictures, and any other items showing the schools' successes should be displayed. This is especially true if the meeting is televised.

All of the board members need to have their packets ready and be dressed professionally. The room should be arrayed in business fashion and have enough seating. Whether on television or not, there needs to be an assigned seat for each staff member who is a regular attendee. This includes the assistant superintendents and directors. Assigned seating is set for the media and other school personnel who come to the meeting. Unless there is a situation in which there is particularly high-level public interest, there should always be enough seats for everyone in attendance. Further, if there is particularly large attendance or a possibility of a conflict, the police should be at the meeting.

What takes place at a board meeting? The schools' business takes place at a board meeting. A school-board meeting is a private meeting held in public. The agenda will have the following sections, or some variation of this:

1. Call to order
2. Invocation
3. Pledge of Allegiance
4. Minutes approved
5. Agenda approved
6. Audience communication
7. Superintendent's report
8. Assistant superintendent's and director's reports
9. Approve bills
10. Approve consent agenda (in some districts this also includes the purchase items)
11. Approve action items
12. Approve personnel items
13. Executive session (if needed)

14. Adjournment

In most states, the first meeting is in July, when a new fiscal year begins and new superintendents take over. It usually consists of normal board items, which include a reorganization of the board, setting of committees, acceptance of bids for the next school year, approving the pay scale for the next school year, and listening to reports of projects completed or ongoing over the summer. The new superintendent will look at the minutes from board meetings that took place a year previously. From these minutes, and with assistance from the board president, the administrative assistant, and central-office administrators, he or she will develop the board agenda.

A superintendent from California said:

> Being a new superintendent with a mandate from the Board to improve student achievement and get the district moving in the right direction, I put into place what was needed for students. We dug into data and identified what was really happening in learning; identified the real gaps and inequities. I also put into place a targeted staff development plan. I hired administrators who were dedicated to children. But I made a major error. I did not cater to the old guard. I was a total failure there.
>
> I had a Board who only supported the superintendent as long as the old guard was happy. They were not happy when the most important thing to me was students. Though I was able to build strong educational teams doing excellent work, I failed at pleasing the old guard. I put the schools and children first. And I did not have a Board committed to their superintendent. The Board's commitment was to the old guard, keeping peace, and status quo. Besides that, being the fourteenth superintendent and the first woman did not make it easier.
>
> I felt my gender was an issue. This was the one aspect I wanted to deny throughout my superintendency. It was the one thing I could not change. I was told by an all-male board to smile more at the old guard, to take notes so they could see that I thought what they said was important. I was told I was flamboyant (I do have short hair and wear colorful clothes). And more importantly, the Board did not trust in my ability to handle the "manly" aspects of my job such as disciplining coaches and building a new high school, though I proved time and time again my knowledge exceeded theirs in those aspects. Gender is an issue I cannot overcome.
>
> I did not make my Board happy since the old guard was unhappy that I did not cater to them. The Board took the move to let the public know that they would not extend my contract nor renew it at its end eighteen months after their announcement. To make it even more difficult, they did not intend to buy me out even though I had done everything they had asked me to accomplish and they approved the direction the district was now moving. Student achievement was up, major program issues had been cleaned up, and accountability had improved. But the Board was not happy. I had failed even though I had not received any corrective directions from the Board. They created a lame-duck superintendent that they were not releasing but expected to continue the work.

I am still superintendent. I am still doing what I have committed to do—the right things for students and staff. The only difference is that I know when this job ends. Inside I am hurt but stand firm. Could I have changed this outcome? Probably. Would I do something different to change the outcome? No. This is the one thing that makes it possible to go to work every day and continue to do the right thing; I am not willing to move outside my values and integrity to appease a dying old guard to the detriment of children.

An Arkansas superintendent said:

I shared enrollment and financial data with the board. I used the same format as the prior superintendent. I added a printout from the online banking so the board could see that the money in the bank balanced with the [state computer network] system. The board did request that the enrollment data be broken out by school, rather than by district, so they could easily detect any trends in student enrollment. The reasoning is that the district is a consolidated school and although it has been twenty-five years since the consolidation, I can detect that resentment still lingers. I also looked back at the prior year's agenda to ensure I was not leaving anything off that the state requires action on by the board.

A new superintendent in Kansas who had just moved up from the deputy-superintendent position responded:

The first meeting went smoothly. It was early June and there was not a lot on the agenda. I did ask the Board to have a work session in mid-July regarding their responsibilities and the superintendent's responsibilities and how they work together. That meeting went very well. I had Dr. "X" come in and provide the training. He was a former superintendent of Kansas City, Kansas Public Schools and now serves in the capacity of consultant work. He took us through several scenarios and asked each of us how we would handle the situation and then followed up with this is how to handle the situation (we found out later that all of the scenarios were based on actual occurrences that he had dealt with in his career).

The Kansas superintendent went on to say:

I did ask the Board to consider shortening the meeting calendar. Previously our Board met twice a month. I asked them to meet twice a month from April to August. These are busy months regarding hiring/firing/budget, etc. and these take place during this time span. In addition, our Board members serve on numerous committees during the school year (mostly September–March) and I wanted to put a premium on them attending these meetings. I told them that was my intent. Attendance by some Board members in previous years was not good and I wanted them to know that good work took place at the "grassroots" committee meetings and the tradeoff would be one Board meeting a month vs. two. They supported my initiative at the Board meeting in July.

A new interim superintendent from Texas said:

> I didn't know that board meetings could be so tense. Three new board members were just elected to the board and you could feel the tenseness in the room. The new members tried to elect their person as the board president. These new members, though their intentions might be honorable, they aren't reading their packet and are asking questions in open session that should be cleared before the meeting. One new board member didn't want a new technology curriculum because she thought there was not enough teacher input. We had never had a K–12 technology before in the district and we're getting close to the start of the school year. She voted against it and I hope she doesn't start to micromanage. We just don't put items on the agenda for our health. We've used committees and have done the research before it is put on the agenda.

From the information supplied by superintendents, it is clear that while school boards may say that they are looking for something/someone different from what they had previously, if there is too much change too quickly the board will not be comfortable. A new superintendent going into a position would do well to research how things were done before and keep some areas of consistency at the first board meeting. No matter how much a group of people say they want a change, it is still difficult. Finding the balance is the trick.

Talking to individuals prior to the meeting and finding out what is most important to each one would be beneficial. During this conversation, bringing up what would have to occur for those changes to take place in a one-on-one setting would help you to gauge the climate for change. If several individuals seem unwilling to do what it takes to make the needed changes, the superintendent may have to take more time for implementation while he or she gets board members and "old guard" on his or her side. One very effective way to get them on your side is to have them come up with the ideas or make them feel as if the needed implementations were their ideas first.

CHECKLIST FOR SCHOOL-BOARD MEETINGS

Davidson (1987) gives some advice as far as working with the board. Here is a checklist developed from the recommendations:

__ Make a visitor sign-in sheet available.

__ Remember the necessity for adequate preparation by superintendent, board members, staff members, press, and citizens.

__ Provide an adequate setting for the meeting. Give attention to details of seating arrangements, acoustics, ventilation, lighting, etc.

__ Provide a competent secretary for recording minutes and a tape record-er for board use. (Note: Today most board meetings are video recorded.)

__ Discuss the atmosphere best suited to your board and the image you wish to project.

__ Look for opportunities for clean humor and wit.

__ Establish a procedure for dealing with groups and organizations ap-pearing before the board. (Note: Most districts have this in policy.)

__ Remember, your primary responsibility concerns the welfare of the students within the school system. (110)

SUMMARY

The first board meeting is the first time the new superintendent and board show how they work together in public. It is usually not an ambitious agenda because a new superintendent's only goal is to take care of necessary items at this meeting. The board will usually not have asked for anything that would stretch the new superintendent, but statements are made that the superintendent knows he or she had better pay attention to. In general, most first board meetings go pretty smoothly.

A board meeting is a private meeting that is done in public. Usually this first board meeting is held in July because that is when most new superintendents start. But superintendents can start anytime during the year—it depends when the positions open. At the first meeting in July, the agenda usually consists of board reorganization, hiring personnel, accepting new contracts, and any last-minute curricular changes. The board meeting follows *Robert's Rules of Order*, and the new superintendent needs to know these rules. This format begins with a call to order and ends with an adjournment. Talking to a few board members in a pre–board meeting conference will help the new superintendent successfully navigate the first board meeting.

REFLECTION QUESTIONS

1. What specific issues has the school board requested that we focus on?
2. What specific issues have been discovered that may need attention on my own?
3. Are any of these areas different? If so, why would they be different? Is it because the board does not want the changes implied in question 2, or because they do not know?
4. Have I spoken with stakeholders to gauge the climate for change in the community, as well as with the board? What were my findings?

5. Do I have individuals who support my ideas, whom I can use as allies for change? Who are these people, and whom do they represent?
6. Are all the changes needed at once, or can I make changes in smaller, less intimidating steps?

Chapter Six

The First Meeting with Supervisory Staff

What kinds of things did you do in your first meeting with your central office staff and/or principals and supervisors? Did they seem intimidated by your expectations? In hindsight, the administrators that seemed most friendly and supportive—did they turn out to really be that way over the next year or two?

Regular supervisory-staff meetings are essential because this allows for the continual communication of the district's vision, goals, and objectives to be discussed while building the team atmosphere. Ramirez (2004) found that within the first ten minutes of meetings, people will decide the kind of relationship they will want to have with the new person. This finding is beneficial because to have an effective team, the new superintendent has to develop relationships.

To complement this, Dunbar, Ramirez, and Burgoon (2003) concluded that the level of participation may be a function of the communication context as well as role relationships. Bob Hagerty, CEO of Polycom, confirmed this finding when interviewed by EffectiveMeetings.com by saying, "When people are engaged, they feel better because they know what's going on, and they can take better and faster action because it's direct information they are getting, not second- or third-hand through some memo that came in the mail or through e-mail" (Smart Technologies editors, 2004).

If you don't talk and listen, then your district will run amok, and it will be like a ship without a rudder. Kinzinger (2007) states that "Well-run staff meetings provide a number of benefits for any organization." He lists nine reasons to hold regular staff meetings, which we have modified to meet the superintendent and district's needs. Regular staff meetings:

1. Contribute to a sense of oneness among co-supervisory staff;
2. Discourage feelings of isolation that can develop when you have only minimal interpersonal communication during the week;
3. Prepare supervisory staff to step in for colleagues when unforeseen absences occur;
4. Stimulate useful ideas about how to deal with problems and how to improve education;
5. Provide a general understanding of what is happening in the school district as a whole and how each supervisor adds value;
6. Reduce friction by giving each supervisor an appropriate forum to air differences and seek resolution;
7. Provide an opportunity for the superintendent to be better informed about all aspects of the school district;
8. Present an excellent forum.
9. Ensure regular and effective communication.

How do you run an effective supervisory-staff meeting? This is a skill, and it's more than just sitting and visiting. The camaraderie built from meetings is nice, but the administrators have jobs they have to do, and their time is precious. Come to the meetings with an agenda and a purpose. Supervisors should know that they have to be prepared, be efficient, and be respectful of everyone's time.

There is no bigger waste of time than a useless meeting. The keys to an effective meeting are detailed planning, understanding the group process, and follow-up/reflection. If the CEO spends that extra time on the front end, the administrators will be comfortable and the meeting will be beneficial. This extra time means that relationships will be built, people will feel like they've been heard, well-thought-out decisions will be made, and administrators will leave with a sense of accomplishment and time well spent. Washington State Department of Health (2003) stipulates the following for a well-thought-out meeting:

A. Plan the agenda and goal.

- Why are you meeting? Write out a clear goal and what you'd like to end up with at the end of the meeting. REMEMBER, to involve staff.
- Gather information and research. Decisions can't be made in the dark and by "the seat of your pants."
- Draft an agenda. This is a road map and a time planner. High priority topics should be at the top of the agenda. Estimate a time limit for each item. REMEMBER, start the agenda out with a welcome and a

time for introductions. And, finally, remember to allow time to review and reflect what you've accomplished, to talk about the next steps and to thank the people for their time.

B. Arrange the logistics.

- Find a comfortable and convenient meeting space. Make certain to arrange in advance for audiovisual equipment or materials such as markers and flip chart, and technology equipment that is needed. Arrive early to make certain everything is ready to go and then greet the people as they arrive.
- Have available beverages and snacks.
- Make sure there are enough comfortable chairs for everyone. Seating arrangement influences the flow of a meeting. Have the chairs set up and decide who sits where. Decide who will be at a table and if you'll have a circle or semicircle. Participants feel more engaged if they are facing each other than if they are sitting in rows.
- Send out the announcement when the meeting is planned. As you get closer to the meeting, send out reminder emails of the date and time with the agenda attached. We would recommend that you send this email out several days before the meeting and then again the day of the meeting. People appreciate the reminders and the copy of the agenda.

C. Keep the discussion on track.

- Your job is a facilitator of the meeting so have your secretary take the minutes or assign it to someone during the first meeting.
- Welcome and introduce the participants and any guests. Sometimes in an administrative staff meeting you might invite a vendor to visit with the principals. You may plan "ice breakers" where each person speaks and gets to know others.
- State the purpose, obtain agreement on the agenda, and set the norms.
- Honor time limits but be sensitive to the need for discussion. If more time is needed for discussion, adjust the agenda. Be gentle but firm with people who want to talk too long.
- Summarize conclusions or decisions as each item is completed.

D. Promote participation and group discussion.

- Plan an activity early in the meeting where each person is asked to contribute in turn. This encourages participation and gets everyone over the hesitancy to speak up.

- Ask open-ended questions, ala [*sic*] Socratic style, and sincerely acknowledge each comment. Make certain you avoid value judgments.
- If someone is dominating simply ask other people for their responses.
- Listen carefully to each person and try to understand what they are saying. Sometimes you'll have to ask them to restate or clarify.
- Use humor as it gets people talking and releases tension.

E. Follow up.

- Your work only begins when the meeting ends. Communicate the group's decision to those who are affected so decisions can be put into action. Send out the minutes to the committee members.

Arneson (2010) recommends an agenda that is simple. It consists of the leader's update (ten–fifteen minutes), team-member round-robin updates (twenty–twenty-five minutes), and big issues (seventy-five minutes). This would be for a two-hour meeting. He argues that staff meetings should be held weekly at the same day and time. Next he says that these meetings should just include the staff, your direct reports. Last, he recommends you adhere to a consistent agenda.

Lang (2000) writes that the meeting style of Fred Bramante, the founder of Daddy's Junky Music, is to always keep his vision of being the best in the industry in front of everybody else in the company. He does this by bringing employees together for staff meetings to discuss where they are and where they should be going. The meetings are able to achieve their objectives because the structure provides an opportunity for everyone to take ownership in the solution, and everyone's input is valued.

Staff meetings can bring out the worst in meetings because there is no flexibility in the time or how often you have them. There are situations that come up in the principal's daily job or a central office administrator's daily job that will dictate the meeting needs to be changed. Another reason for bringing out the worst is that you don't want to face a "thorn in the flesh" or a combative colleague. A third reason is putting up with chronic complainers and bullying colleagues. A fourth reason is that the meeting is a waste of time as the colleagues and boss could start acting childish and disrupting others. An example of this is: Trying to joke about what is going on or playing pranks. A fourth reason is that some colleagues try to be dominate over others. A fifth reason is that this demonstrates the school or school district is dysfunctional.

Toback (2009) says, "Meetings are hard enough to do effectively, but weekly meetings can be the hardest. Why, I don't know. But in my experience, most principals and other administrators are so inept at conducting

Will this be a formal meeting, or an informal time to get to know each other?
If I have already met them, what might I need to do to establish trust and communication with them that I have not already done?
Are there any staff members that I need to prep before the meeting? Why?
You are going to train your staff on what you expect in staff meetings. Decide how you will design that in-services and a "staff meeting protocol" in-service.
Describe what you will do to gather buy-in from the supervisory staff. What will you do to develop the team atmosphere?

effective meetings you'd think it's rocket science or a rare genetic trait." Toback has given some very good advice; but for a superintendent, weekly meetings are essential.

Superintendents set the ethical tone of their districts. This comes from the first meeting, in which the superintendent talks about the code of ethics and what is legal. This ethics code should cover conflicts of interest, self-dealing, gifts, sexual harassment, and outside employment. It should prohibit political contributions, service on for-profit boards, and the use of confidential information for personal gain. The challenge is to promote the district's values.

"In my first meeting, I told them about my philosophy and vision for the district," said one superintendent we polled. "They did react a little like they were intimidated by my expectations. The administrators that initially seemed most friendly and supportive really turned out that way about 50-50."

A superintendent in western Arkansas said:

> I was privileged to hire a new high school principal the first year I was superintendent. He has worked out well, is extremely supportive, as is the elementary principal. They both present at the annual report to the public and are eager to please. We are the only three administrators and all work well together to accomplish what is requested by state/federal mandates. We have worked together going on three years, and they are still as eager to please and work hard as they were the very first year. They never appeared intimidated by my expectations. The central office staff did not play a part in the meeting, other than the district treasurer takes minutes at the meetings.
> My first meetings were about establishing trust and lines of communication. I didn't start talking about expectations for a few months. I have taken a "human" approach to building relationships as opposed to a "do this or else" approach. In retrospect, the first impression I had of people has generally held true.

A Kansas superintendent said:

> I remember our first meeting with the "new" staff (directors) was on July 12. I had just returned from vacation and others were getting ready to leave. This was the one day in the month where we had all of us present (only one was gone). We talked about goals, expectations, support, and roles. It was a good meeting. The new staff were exposed to the returning staff and it was a good "ice-breaker" meeting.

The *Americus (GA) Times-Recorder* reported on the first meeting of a superintendent's cabinet:

> During his first month as new superintendent of Sumter County Schools, Roy Brooks has orchestrated meetings with many different school personnel and community leaders. At the first meeting of his Cabinet, Brooks presented an

agenda of acceptable procedure for proper introduction of management concern. The vision for the Cabinet is, "The Sumter county School District will be among the highest achieving rural school districts in Georgia."

On the agenda was Brooks' rule of management—"Give people the authority, give them the responsibility, give them the resources and then make them accountable for the results." Before addressing the first agenda, Brooks shared,

> "The community looks at the building and grounds, then they look at the test scores, and they make the decision to take their children somewhere else based on their initial impression. We are losing hundreds of students, and millions of dollars, because some of our schools are not competitive academically and some of our schools and grounds look neglected and rundown.
>
> Some of our schools and central office departments are not providing the highest level of customer service. We must realize that students, taxpayers, and this community deserve better."

On this first action agenda were 11 items: board meeting agenda items, weekly updates, no surprise updates, student learning, personnel services, schedule of meeting dates, out of pocket notification, transportation, maintenance, finance, and project management were discussed at the conclusion of the hour-long meeting. ("First Meeting" 2010)

Referencing the data from the panel of superintendents, it was interesting that this question was one of the least answered questions. That leads to several questions. Did respondents skip the question because the first meeting with the supervisory staff was informal and did not leave a lasting impression? Did the meetings not go well? Did the superintendent recognize the value of this first meeting? All of these are questions that need to be addressed.

For a new person in the school district, the supervisory staff that is already in place can be the biggest asset or biggest liability. As much as the staff needs to make a good impression, the CEO needs to do the same as well. As one of the respondents mentioned, establishing trust and lines of communication is very important. The importance of this cannot be downplayed. This is probably as important as, or even more important than, getting your expectations of what you want them to do in the coming year.

Without trust, you will not have your staff supporting you. They may be suspicious of your ideas and motives. Therefore, one would do well to work on the personal, "human" aspects to building a sound relationship before creating demands. It all comes down to the fact that we are dealing with human beings who are just as nervous about you coming in as you are about coming in as a new superintendent.

CHECKLIST FOR THE FIRST MEETING WITH THE SUPERVISORY STAFF

__ Room is reserved, is prepared with seating, and has all needed equipment.

__ Heating, air, lighting, and ventilation have bee

__ Beverages and snacks are prepared and ready.

__ Napkins, paper plates, plastic utensils are prov

__ Agenda is prepared and printed for individuals

__ Specific questions and activities have been plar

__ Other print materials are prepared.

__ Notification of meeting was made prior to me other notification media.

__ Attendees are communicated with one day prior

__ Anything else that is needed for the meeting has

__ Ice-breaker is used to develop team atmosphere.

__ Staff are welcomed as they arrive.

__ Meeting is informative, friendly, and the right ler

2.

3.

4.

5.

6.

SUMMARY

Regular supervisory-staff meetings are necessary as thi tinual communication of the district's vision, goals, ar can be discussed while building the team atmosphere. A ry-staff meeting, it's important that the superintendent listen, then your district will run amok and problems will

The keys to an effective meeting are detailed planning group process, and follow-up/reflection. Finally, superint cal tone of their districts. This comes from the first me superintendent talks about the code of ethics and what from the responses, the first meeting consisted of commu intendent's philosophy and vision for the district. Intimid your expectations, and so it's essential to build the team atr

Most superintendents felt that half of the supervisory sta of them and the other half just observant. The superviso superintendent's biggest asset or biggest liability and car successfully through your first supervisory-staff meeting. staff needs to make a good impression, the superintendent same. Establishing trust and lines of communication is ver this cannot be stressed strongly enough.

REFLECTION QUESTIONS

1. Have I prepared for and planned for making my first my supervisory staff?

Chapter Seven

What was the First Encounter with an Angry Parent or Patron Like?

What was the first encounter with an angry parent or patron like? Had the parent gone through the chain of command before coming to you? Did the parent or patron seem to be playing craftily with you to try to get you to make a classic upper-management mistake? Describe this.

The patron called to tell me that her child had missed the bus and she was just going nuts—screaming, hollering over the phone. She would not listen long enough for me to ask her what her physical address was or to even get her child's name. She came into the office a couple of days later and apologized. She had found a note in her child's backpack describing a change in the regular bus route. Her child did not wait long enough at the bus stop in order to catch the bus.

The above description from a superintendent in Arkansas personifies exactly what a beginning superintendent would rather *not* face.

In the business of education you will have the opportunity to meet an angry parent. We have their most precious item, their child, in our care, and they demand the best for "little junior." In addition, many parents are very involved at the schools, through everything from the parent-teacher association to the athletic booster club. As Kaatz (2007) succinctly puts it, "One encounter with a hostile parent can blot out dozens of positive, helpful meetings" (1).

Another questionnaire response described an experience as follows:

> Dealing with my first angry parent was similar to situations I had experienced
> in the principalship. The parent had gone through the chain of command
> before getting to me. This parent seemed to be looking out for his child instead
> of trying to play clever administrative games. Sometimes that viewpoint dif-
> fers greatly for the district's view of what is best for all students.

Another superintendent responded, "The first parent I talked to was 'under-
medicated' and 'out-of-it.' She didn't want to follow the chain of command
and didn't understand district protocol."

What are situations that cause a parent to become angry with the superintendent? Table 7.1 lists a sample of newspaper articles about parent anger
aimed at the superintendent and board. The question could be asked: What
causes this anger? Judging from table 7.1, anger arose with respect to inappropriate physicals, bullying, class placement, compensation packages, the
future of the district, audit reports, changes in boundaries, and asbestos concerns.

These are just a sample of issues that cause parents to get angry. When
parents feel as if their children will be harmed, injured, or put at a disadvan-
tage, they will become angry. If they feel the district is not representing their
values and community, they will get angry.

The daily stresses of life in our current fast-paced world, which are a
cause of anger, propel parents to reach their "boiling point." When this
happens they will lash out at whoever they feel is responsible for their anxiety or problem.

There's not an easy answer to the question of why parents become angry.
Things are going on in parents' lives, and they have their reasons. The angry
parent comes from all walks of life. Kaatz, cited in Seligman (2000), identifies angry parents by characteristics that range from hostility to neglect. He
also notes that a family may look stable on the outside but for whatever
reason may have encountered numerous stressors in their lives that make
them angry and hostile.

Seligman (2000) observes, "It may sometimes be difficult to determine
whether a parent's angry behavior and remarks can be taken at face value or
whether they are manifestations of unconscious feelings related to factors
unknown to the parents" (227). Jaksec (2005) says that parents may become
hostile because they are not familiar with the school. This lack of familiarity
is tied directly to school-home communications.

According to Pritchardt (2003), a parent can become angry for several
different reasons:

> Some people have more of a genetic make-up to get angry easily. Some people
> are under more stress than others or are going through stressful times in their
> lives. Anger also occurs more often with a lack of sleep and not eating proper-

Table 7.1. Newspaper articles headlining angry-parent concerns

Headline	Source and Date
a. Charges expected soon for inappropriate physicals, Highline superintendents tells angry parents.	a) *Highline Times* June 6, 2010
b. Angry parents confront school board with tales of bullying.	b) WFBF News
c. New York superintendent wrestles gun away from angry parent.	October 13, 2010
d. Location, location, location: Parents, superintendent exchange words over pre-K placement.	c) KSDK.com October 18, 2010
e. Parents complain CFISD isn't doing enough to stop bullying.	d) *Hudson*
f. A letter to the new superintendent about Georgia having the lowest level of expectations and to get in "the driver's seat."	*Reporter* August 22, 2010
g. Parents are angry over the superintendent's additional retirement package.	e) KHOU TV October 6, 2010
h. Angry parents told district must focus on the future.	f) AJC June 24, 2010
i. At last Lee County school district bus audit released.	g) *Oregonian*Octob
j. Former superintendent interview on her tenure at Del Mar Union School District.	er 17, 2010
k. Leonia school superintendent holds session with parents over asbestos concerns.	h) *Arizona Republic* October 31, 2007
	i) Florida Fox 4 News September 9, 2010
	j) *Del Mar Times* May 13, 2010
	k) NewJersey.com May 24, 2010

ly. An event that sets off anger today might not tomorrow. Statistics indicate that women who are stressed tend to go into a depression while men who are stressed tend to get angry. A pressure situation can cause an average woman to get depressed but the same situation causes the average man to become an angry father. Some of parents' anger is correlated to the psychological make-up of a person. . . . Men are especially prone to feeling disrespected. Frustration during times of helplessness or powerlessness can cause an angry dad. (1)

Prickhardt (2003) identifies several reasons why parents get angry (table 7.2).

Another reason for parents' anger can be that they have an erroneous perception of the school. What the parents expect and what the school personnel expect may be two different things. Kaatz (2003) concludes that administrators believe parents want them to act professionally. Parents complain that administrators are condescending and patronizing. What parents really wanted is an administrator who is a "servant leader."

Table 7.2. Reasons for anger

Reasons Why Parents Get Angry

1. Parents who have a HIGH NEED TO CONTROL will often get mad when they don't get their way or don't get what they want right away.
2. Parents who are HIGHLY JUDGMENTAL will often get mad when others contradict their opinions or don't do things the "right" way.
3. Parents who have a HIGH SENSITIVITY TO HURT will often get mad when they take slights or offenses personally that were not personally meant.
4. Parents who have a HIGH NEED FOR GRIEVANCE will often get mad when they use being wronged to justify nursing a grudge to sustain resentment.
5. Parents who have a HIGH NEED TO INTIMIDATE will often get mad when they want to bully other people with their anger.

According to Greenleaf (1977), a *servant leader* is a person in authority who is deserving of allegiance because power from the follower is "freely and knowingly granted by the led to the leader in response to, and in proportion to, the clearly evident servant stature of the leader" (25). Thus, if the parents do not feel the superintendent is "serving" them or their needs, they will be unwilling to support him or her as their leader. Lindle (1989) concluded from her research on what parents wanted from an administrator that an "administrator's attitude and personal characteristics were also considered paramount" (Jaksec 2000, 21).

Superintendents work with parents who are "troubled, afraid, or just . . . crazy" (McEwan 1998). Dealing with angry parents is not unique to American schools. In Japan, staff are hired to deal with "monster parents" (Kaatz 2007).

To be an effective superintendent, one has to grow thick "mule skin" (Rosberg, McGee, and Burgett 2007) and become "hard of hearing." That is, "hard of hearing" with respect to the accusations and anger thrown at one. Ignorant people sometimes do not comprehend or appreciate what administrators are doing for them. Rosberg, McGee, and Burgett say:

> In the education business, administrators deal with many people, each with his/her own opinion about schools. Not all of those opinions concur. Consequently, parents will get angry with the superintendent about a decision that is made. Nothing good is accomplished when the parent and superintendent are in an emotional state. The superintendent's responsibility is to remain professional, calm, and look beyond the situation. Questions must be asked, like "Why is this parent acting like this?" "Is something else going on in his/her life that is dictating this behavior?" (7–8)

Table 7.3 (Kaatz et al. 2007) lists things to do and not to do when dealing with angry parents.

Defusing anger is part of a superintendent's job. Ask the parents if they are mad at you or the situation. Many times this will help the parents calm down. An administrator, when meeting with angry parents, should never lose his or her temper, as this is comparable to "pouring gasoline on a fire." No matter what, don't get angry, and politely ask them to cool down. If the parent cannot calm down, ask him or her to make an appointment to see you later. If the parent does calm down, calmly ask him or her to continue.

Take notes, and only interrupt for clarification. Wait until the person is finished, then restate what was said to make sure that both of you are in accord. From there, an opportunity to problem-solve takes place. This makes you, the superintendent, the problem solver.

Most people are excellent problem identifiers, but very few are problem solvers. Patience and "mule skin" pay off in problem solving. Dimperio (1996) anticipated Rosberg, McGee, and Burgett (2007) when he identified several strategies that could help superintendents deal with angry people over the phone, during school visits, or at public meetings. He recommends that·

- You don't take it personally.
- Try to obtain the information as quickly as possible. The objective is to get the angry parent out of the office or off the phone, but support staff never should hang up on a caller.
- Don't get angry or argue. That can be a trap.
- Don't use humor unless you are sure it is appropriate as it can be taken the wrong way.
- Acknowledge you are concerned and empathize.
- Return calls promptly.
- Direct the caller appropriately.
- Don't exceed your authority.
- Stay calm.

Dimperio (1996) says that "it is important to realize that some parents' anger is based on a frustrating experience they had in school. Our role is to help, and we need to learn how to handle a problem without getting angry or hostile. By responding with kindness and concern, we show that in our school district people don't have to get angry to get attention" (2). In Proverbs 15:1, King Solomon says, "A gentle answer turns away wrath." This advice is echoed by O'Donovan (2007) when he summarizes a training session hosted by a communications specialist. Her advice to administrators included the following points:

- Let people have their say without interruption. This venting is necessary to allow the administrator to move to a solution.
- Express empathy for the ideas shared. You don't have to agree.

Table 7.3. Things "to do" and "not to do" when dealing with angry parents

The "DO" List

- Begin with a warm hand-shake and welcome.
- Listen, and listen some more.
- Focus on the problem, not personality.
- Ask how the situation can be improved; apologize if in the wrong.
- Make only those promises you can keep.
- Use practical suggestions from parents as a springboard for action.
- Remember that parental anger may be due to interaction with a specific staff member.
- Suggest a neutral place to meet if your feel the parent is hostile to *everything*. A neutral location could be a coffee shop, food court, or a community center.
- Emphasize the "we" in the situation: "We all want what's best for Tom." "What do you think we can do to deal with this problem?"
- Document, document, document; if an incident is not documented, it DID NOT happen.
- Many angry parents want a listening ear as much as, if not more than, they want answers, SO LISTEN.
- Whether in person or on the phone, all encounters with angry parents should be handled with wisdom and tact. Remember, "you can catch more flies with honey than you can with vinegar."

Things "NOT TO DO"

- Take the parent's anger personally.
- Attribute motives to the parents. There are probably factors you know nothing about.
- Defend yourself before the parents are finished speaking. The very act of becoming defensive impedes communication.
- Believe that you have to meet "right away" at the parent's insistence. Delaying will allow you to collect information and let the parent cool.
- Meet with the parents by yourself if you are afraid of them or want additional administrative backing, moral support, or someone to take notes. Having another person attend the meeting is perfectly acceptable.
- Be afraid to terminate the conference if the parent becomes verbally abusive or appears to be on the verge of a physical attack.
- Arrange the seating so that the parent is between you and the door.
- Have a meeting in an isolated area of the building.
- Meet alone with parents when everyone else has left the building.
- Be afraid to show the parents any notes you have taken about the meeting.
- Get sidetracked. Don't let the parent steer the conversation to negative comments about other parents or employees. Keep on the subject.
- Forget the words of an administrator of a public school in Missouri, "...most people get glad in the same pants they were mad in" (*Education World*, n.d.).
- Be afraid to apologize if you made a mistake that might make a parent justifiably angry.

Kaatz et al. (2003)

- Avoid a standoff. Move around obstacles to focus on what you can do.
- Suggest solutions and affirm the steps you will take.
- Follow through on what you agreed.

Cupitt's (2009) tips for dealing with angry parents are listed in table 7.4.

Kaatz (2007) lists four methods to use when dealing with angry parents. Table 7.5 lists these methods. These methods echo a nondirective mode of counseling.

Schools need to be proactive and parent friendly. The following recommendations are modified from *Building Parent Partnerships* (Gutloff 1966):

- Sponsor parent-child or parent-faculty kickball or softball games, or other sporting events.
- Open the gym at least one night a week for family recreation night.
- In elementary school, invite parents to read a favorite book or chapter to the students.
- Create a "parent university" that might use staff and parent expertise to teach classes about computers, gardening, or physical fitness, or offer parenting classes on issues like teenage development, drug-use prevention, bullying, spirituality in children, and so forth. Parents can be invited to be the "professors" in this "university."
- Have a "parent talent night" during the school year to allow parents to showcase their talent.
- Allow students to invite parents or other family members into their classrooms for part of the day.

Table 7.4. Tips for dealing with angry parents

Tips on Dealing with Angry or Difficult Parents

1. Get back to the parent as soon as possible.
2. Listen without interruption.
3. Don't take the complaint personally; remain mentally detached.
4. Ask non-threatening questions when trying to determine the problem.
5. Bring up some similar situation that can help place you on the same level as the parent you are talking to.
6. Call parents by their names. Never use the first name unless you are personally acquainted.
7. Ask parents exactly what they want, if they have not already told you.
8. Don't get into a shouting match.
9. Apologize if needed.

Cupitt (2009)

Table 7.5. Methods to use when dealing with angry parents

Methods	Description
SODAS	*State* the problem; list the possible *Options* to deal with the problem; for each option discuss the *Disadvantages* and the *Advantages*, and then *Select* one or more of the options.
LEAP	**L** – Listen actively **E**—Empathize. You must acknowledge the parents' feelings and make the parents feel their complaint is being heard. **A** – Ask questions. This also helps the parent feel their complaints are being taken seriously and it allows you to see their viewpoint. This can diffuse the parent's anger. **P** – Problem solve. Here is where you can ask questions like, "What do you think we can do about the situation?" "What would you like me to do?" "What are your ideas about a plan we can work out together?" "How do you want me to report back to you?"
STRIDE	**Status.** Begin with the situation as it exists; what is exactly the current **Status**? These questions will help you find the current Status: *What is happening now that we would like to change?* *Give a tangible example of the problem?* *Who owns the problem?* **Target** of the change. Sample questions to ask are: *What will the hallways be like if we fix this?* *Who will benefit from reducing the amount of bullying?* *How can those who benefit be involved in hitting the target?* **Restraining** forces. Sample questions to ask are: *Why does the problem with bullying continue?* *Is there a reason this has not been addressed before?* *What is working for and what is working against solving the problems?* **Identify** the issues that are restraining movement to solve the problem. **Decision** time. What do you agree to do? **Evaluation.** How will we measure success?
RAID	Jaksec (2005) recommends that this approach is meant as an option prior to the formal meeting. **Recognize** the potential for a violent encounter. **Assess** your ability to handle the situation. **Diffuse** the parent's anger during the initial approach and greeting. If the eye contact is not returned and the handshake refused, then you already have some important information. You still thank the parent for coming to the meeting even if it was their idea.

Kaatz (2003)

We recommend that you list in the school personnel policy manual policies on how to handle verbally or physically abusive parents. Place within the manual a form that the parent signs that says the parent has read the handbook. Arguing with a parent is like "shooting yourself in the foot." Instead of arguing, coopt with the parent. Find a skill the parent has, and then invite this parent to become involved in the school.

Another idea is to have *posi-calls*, which means requiring the staff to call the parent twice a month about their children and positive news. During in-service days, utilize role-playing minisessions using the methods shown in table 7.4. Other proactive methods are evening office hours once a month, memorandums of agreement, providing parents with positive school experiences as soon as their children enroll, and so forth. The gist is to have the parents experience school as a positive place that is there for the well-being of their children.

Schultz (2005) says that his first encounter with an angry parent was when he received an angry phone message asking why the school hired criminals. He called the parent back and tried to explain that it was a county park issue and not a school issue, and it was out of his control. It didn't matter to the parent who was in control; he was the superintendent and should have taken care of the problem. Schultz learned the following from this lesson: *the buck stops here, even when you have no control.*

One of our respondents wrote that:

> My first encounter with an angry parent was when the president of the local NAACP showed up in my office with a very angry parent and her entourage. She had earlier visited with the building principal but skipped the remaining steps in the "chain of command." She had brought along her husband, her two sisters, and the president of the NAACP. She was, to put it mildly, livid with an elementary principal. She in no uncertain terms told me that her son is not going to be treated unfairly and that they weren't going to put up with it anymore. She accused the principal of racially discriminating against her son and she wanted the principal fired.
>
> I followed all of the recommended suggestions from the above researchers to calm this lady down but she would not be calmed down. I invited the party in to sit down, offered them coffee or water, and then calmly asked them what I could do for them and help them. She went off in a rant. I just listened. As she was talking I asked the assistant superintendent to come in, not for support but for a possible solution.
>
> The president of the NAACP tried talking to her and they discussed in a very vigorous way what was happening and how to fix the problem. After three hours of listening we offered a solution, which the mother's husband and the president of the NAACP agreed upon. The mother was not in agreement but because her support group supported the solution, she agreed and stomped out of the office. Our solution was to transfer the student to another elementary school in which we had a specially assigned teacher for that student.

The building principal was in agreement and we transferred the student. At the end of the year, I ran into the parent and her countenance had changed. She told me that this was the best year her son ever had. The difference was that she felt someone finally truly cared for and helped her son. I can't say all my encounters with angry parents ended up positively. But this first encounter did. You never know what will set a parent off.

In regards to the question, "Did the parent play craftily with me . . . ?" I felt the parent was so angry that they weren't thinking about playing games. What I had to do was to make certain I didn't say anything or do anything that would hinder the solution. This is crucial because we, as administrators, also have emotions and we have to keep them under control. Calmness and tact are the keys.

From another respondent:

I remember an angry parent came to a board meeting when I was a superintendent in Minnesota. I was embarrassed as the parent was quite vocal in open meeting. (There was no chain of command followed here . . . straight to the Board of Education.) The parent was angry about the school bus pick-up area and felt that his child was in danger where she had to get on the bus.

The parent wanted the bus to drive down into his driveway to pick up his child. I met with the parent after the meeting and made arrangements to come out to his house to see where his child was picked up. I also told him we would drive the bus route together so the parent could visually see the route. When we arrived back to his house, he still wanted to have the bus come into his driveway but because I took the time and drove the route with him, his anger was abated, and we never had problems from him again.

In following the chain of command, I rarely had an angry parent come directly to the Board of Education to visit with me. Usually they had visited with the building principal. When they felt they didn't get relief, then the angry parent would "leap-frog" the directors and assistant superintendents and come straight to me. My secretary was very good about getting the angry parent to calm down and then direct them to the proper office.

My experiences of parents not following the chain of command were through phone calls. I would calmly listen to their complaint and then ask them if they had visited with the teacher or building principal. If they had, I would ask them for time so I could look into the matter and then I would either have the building principal call back or the assistant superintendent.

If I had a phone message from an angry parent, I immediately called the building principal and asked that they solve that problem. Ninety-nine percent of the time the problem was solved by the building principal. Usually the principal didn't even know a problem existed and said something like this, "All they had to do was call me and we could have solved this problem."

These stories that this respondent told all relate back to the superintendent's need to be patient and calm, to follow specific guidelines previously discussed, and to follow the chain of command within the district. This can be by utilizing the following questions and statements:

- "Have you visited with your building principal or teacher?"
- "After you visit with them, if the problem isn't solved, would you please make an appointment with the assistant superintendent to work this problem out?
- "I need to look into this matter, and either I myself or a designee will get back with you in a very timely manner."

Remember, in dealing with angry parents, stay calm, show concern and empathy, actively seek a solution, and get back in touch with them in a very timely manner. Show as much care and concern as if it were your own child. We are their "servants"; and remember the Walmart attitude, "the customer is always right."

CHECKLIST FOR A MEETING WITH AN ANGRY PARENT

__ Review steps on how to deal with angry parents.
__ Prepare for meeting by using a method described in table 7.5.
__ Make sure your office is clean and inviting.
__ Welcome the parents with a firm handshake.
__ Use the parents' names when visiting with them (but not their first names unless you know them).
__ Sit in front of the desk with the parents so there is no barrier.
__ Offer water, tea, coffee, or soda to the parents.
__ Treat the parents respectfully.
__ Exhibit friendliness, empathy, and concern.
__ Listen, Listen, Listen, and make eye contact.
__ Keep a calm demeanor.
__ Talk softly and keep voice calm.
__ Invite the parents to share their concerns.
__ Clarify what you heard.
__ Summarize what you heard.
__ Schedule another meeting if needed.
__ Conclude with a solution and on an open invitation.
__ Walk the parents to the door.
__ Reflect on improvement.
__ Engage in continual professional-development training and scenarios with follow-up.
__ Fulfill the district's mission statement.

SUMMARY

Angry parents like to "leap-frog" the chain of command as they want action immediately. Follow the "do" and "not to do" list that is found in table 7.3. Understand reasons that parents get angry and then prepare for the meeting, if possible. If the parent just shows up, listen, listen, listen, then invite him or her back in a timely fashion for a follow-up meeting. This will allow you time to get to the bottom of the problem. Utilize one of the methods in table 7.5 (Sodas, Leap, Stride, Raid).

Remember, the parent or patron who comes to your office to vent anger is likely not at his or her best. He or she will look back on that moment later and reflect on how foolish the outburst was. Recognize that the anger is an expression of weakness, not of overpowering strength.

In most cases, the complainant is someone who under different circumstances might be a good friend and ally. Avoid burning bridges, as you may need to cross over them again. Treat the parent like you would like to be treated. Approaching leadership with a true servant attitude is a big head start on controlling anger.

Become acquainted with one or more of the methods listed above for defusing your own anger. Find ways to not let the adrenaline flow. Being able to control the adrenaline when ordinary people would have let the situation get to them is the mark of a mature person and a true professional. Not many people can do this.

REFLECTION QUESTIONS

1. Do I have questions prepared to be able to find out necessary information to handle situations?
2. Have I made out a mental plan for dealing with irrational individuals?
3. How have I organized my office to protect staff and/or myself in the event that I have a violent parent?
4. Go over scenarios with your supervisory staff by role-playing. This will allow you to feel the situation and think about the situation. Critique each participant.
5. How does calming an angry parent benefit the school district, school, parent, and student?
6. Design your office for these encounters. Have it critiqued by other supervisors.
7. Why is it crucial to solve these problems and defuse the anger in a positive manner? What are the benefits to the district?

8. What does your body experience, physically, when you have angry/ tense encounters with parents?

Chapter Eight

School Property and the Proprietary Role

Renting/leasing school property and buying property: How successful were you in keeping your district out of the proprietary role in sharing facilities with the community?

School districts take on a proprietary role because of such factors as decreasing/increasing student populations, disasters that occur, the selling of district land, the purchasing of land for the district, or the leasing/renting of facilities to community groups. It is important for the superintendent to remember that schools are in the business of education and not let the proprietary role overshadow the school's main function. If this role overshadows education, then this will be sending a bad message to the community, like *the school is more interested in business than students learning.*

Although the above question was posed to twenty-four superintendents from twelve states, hailing from a number of universities, very few of them seemed to be able to speak to the issues of school property and the proprietary role. One said, "Not sure I understand this question." Possibly the question had a legal term in it that the respondents did not recognize. But a topic that has been to court at least eight times, and that could result in the forfeiture of sovereign immunity, is not one that should be easily dismissed.

The concept of the *proprietary role* could have enormous legal implications to boards, leadership teams, and teachers. In this chapter, we will attempt to enlighten readers about the issue of proprietary role. In *Reutter's The Law of Public Education*, 5th ed., Russo (2004) draws two defining lines between a normal (protected) operation of school facilities and proprietary use: (1) "the actual and intended result of the funds collected for renting or leasing school property is for recovering expenses associated with that use," and (2) "whether the activity was within a customary curricular use of a school district within the state."

In *Sawaya v. Tucson*, the Arizona Supreme Court declared that when a district rented its property (in this case a football stadium) to another entity and made even a small profit while doing so, the school district lost its sovereign immunity and was liable for a spectator's injury. With *sovereign immunity*, the school is protected from lawsuits that arise from an individual's behavior. Without it, if there is a mishap involving tort liability during the time that the district has taken on what the court called a *proprietary role*, the district may be sued for negligence. (See also *Richards v. School District of Birmingham, Michigan.*)

It is the nature of such events that the timing could not be worse for the district to lose its sovereign protection than at a point of high risk for litigation over negligence. The risks associated with proprietary role may be elevated if a private business in the district loses business because the school district has thereby gone into competition with it. The classic case would be that of renting a school cafeteria to 4-H, Kiwanis, Rotary, Lion's Club, or some other such group.

A district could simply say that it will not rent school facilities to any organization. If the district does choose to rent cafeterias, gymnasiums, band halls, stadiums, and so on to organizations, there should be definite policies established about those usages, and fees set at a level that will enable the district to pay for the increased maintenance.

In many small towns, the cafeteria is the eating establishment that feeds the greatest number of people lunch on weekdays. Hence the cafeteria has the equipment and the capability to feed a large number of people. It might be one thing if the school rented its cafeteria one night per month to one organization, at cost. When it begins to rent very often, it has an impact on the commercial eating establishments in town.

If a school cafeteria's hot-water heater explodes during one of those chili suppers and the local eating establishments have had enough of the competition that the school is creating for them, they may find this to be an opportune time to support a lawsuit against the school for negligence—and the district could find itself in a proprietary role at exactly the time it needed to be protected under sovereign immunity.

One district stated its policy for use of facilities as follows:

USE OF SCHOOL FACILITIES

I. Community Organizations

(School facilities shall be available for use by community organizations when such use does not interfere with the regular school program and provided that all expenses incurred in the use of these facilities are borne by the organizations using them. If the representatives of such organizations do not exercise sound judgment or do not provide close supervision for the activity, such use may be denied. "Schedule of Charges for Use of School Buildings and Facilities")

II. Payment of Fees for Use of Buildings and Facilities

Subject to conditions named elsewhere in these rules, and upon payment of charges in advance as set forth in the schedule of charges, certain parts of the school buildings, grounds, and athletic fields of the Russellville School District may be used by organizations or groups for meetings intended for recreation, self-improvement, or community improvement, and by local congregations of churches on a temporary basis in cases of emergencies or catastrophes, only.

III. Use of School Buildings by Red Cross in Event of Disaster

The Superintendent of Schools, Assistant Superintendent, and a member of the Red Cross shall be the committee to decide when a disaster exists and when the schools are needed for this purpose. Notification to principals and the Food Service Department shall come from the Central Office. Public school buildings will be used only in cases of major disasters such as bombings, tornadoes, etc.

IV. Uses of Buildings Not Allowed

No meeting will be held in a school building for the purpose of advancing any doctrine or theory subversive to the Constitution or laws of the state of Arkansas or the United States; promotion of private profit-making enterprises; or any entertainment that may be detrimental or destructive to the buildings, fixtures, or furniture.

Most school districts utilize this type of policy, which dictates how the district can allow outside public use of the facilities. Liberal USD 480, in Liberal, Kansas, has written into its policy the following sentence: "The superintendent has authority to manage the district's business affairs." This statement was designed to prevent minor requests from coming before the board and to give the superintendent the freedom to make these decisions.

Another policy that needs to be in place is one regarding transportation. Different groups will come and ask to use a school bus. Either state law or district policy will dictate your response. Liberal USD 480 has two policies that cover this area. These are known as EDAA and EDDA, and they read as follows:

EDAA: School Vehicles

School buses will not be loaned, leased or subcontracted to any person, groups of persons or organizations except as allowed by law subject to board approval.

No school vehicle of any type shall be used by any student, school employee, patron or any organization to transport anyone to or from a religious activity.

No public funds will be spent by the board to hire, rent or lease any form of transportation to be used by any student, school employee, patron or any organization to transport anyone to or from a religious activity.

EDDA: School Use of School Buses

The board may allow for special uses of district buses using guidelines established in this policy. Transportation fees may be charged to offset totally or in part the cost of approved special trips. Revenues received by the board under the provisions of this policy shall not be considered a reduction of operating expenses of the school district.

Groups allowed use of buses under this policy are responsible for the care and cleaning of the buses, and for the supervision of passengers. The types of groups allowed, and the restrictions placed on the activities these groups may sponsor while using district transportation, shall be approved by the board and filed with the clerk. Groups traveling outside of Kansas will be limited to 300 miles one way. Exceptions may be granted by the Superintendent or his designee.

The board desired that the superintendent use integrity, frugality, economical sense, and business sense in making the decision to lease, use, or rent school property by adding this sentence into a policy: "The district's business affairs shall be managed in the most economical and efficient manner possible."

In the spring of 2011 an F-5 tornado hit Joplin, Missouri, and demolished the high school. The high school was able to reopen on time, as the school rented a portion of the mall. Kelsey Ryan of the *Joplin Globe* reported, "The Joplin School District opened its new term Wednesday—87 days after being stunned by an EF-5 tornado—with no major hitches, officials said. Some principals declared this year's first day of school, even in an array of temporary locations, one of the smoothest ever."

Ray, Candoli, and Hack (2005) concluded that rental of facilities is effective, especially when there is need for more school rooms because of population projections or, as described above, when a disaster has destroyed a building. In some instances, facilities can be shared with other agencies. Some businesses will provide facilities in return for the school system operating a school to service their employees.

In Durant, Oklahoma, the facilities policies are near the end of their online policy manual. They are posted at www.durantisd.org/admin/board/policy/disd_policy-g.pdf and read much like those printed above, from a school district in Arkansas. The Bryan (Texas) Independent School District policies on facilities usage state explicitly that fees should not exceed the actual cost of making the facility available to the public. It also has the forms necessary for an entity such as the Boy Scouts to request the use of a class-room, gymnasium, or building, which are found at www.tasb.org/policy/pol/private/021902/pol.cfm?DisplayPage=GKD(LEGAL).pdf. "It is common for our community to use school facilities," said one Arkansas superintendent. "There is a Facilities Use form which basically asks for the name of the organization, time, data, building, and what equipment is needed, if any."

Today, it is imperative that the school district share their facilities with the community. In Broken Arrow, Oklahoma, after the school day is over, the school is used for community education. In Liberal, Kansas, the gyms are used by youth leagues and other facilities are used by groups requesting their usage. This is seen as a duty because the building is the community's and should be utilized.

The superintendent who makes a unilateral decision to deny the use of a school building, without first taking that request to the board, will be a short-term superintendent. All of the superintendents we visited with either fol-lowed district policy in regard to this matter or didn't quite understand the question.

CHECKLIST

__ Update building-usage policies.

__ Update transportation-usage policies.

__ Board is informed of the policies and if any changes need to be made.

__ Administrators, teachers, and support have been provided the school-property usage policy.

__ School-usage policy is in faculty and administrator handbook.

__ School attorney has been contacted to make certain the policy coin-cides with state law.

__ Updates have been placed on the board agenda and adopted by the board.

__ Policies are updated and amended periodically.

__ Mission statement demonstrates that the district values education over proprietary revenues.

SUMMARY

If a district takes on a proprietary role, it can have negative connotations and signal to the community that the district is more interested in the business side of education than the educating side of education. There are several valid reasons why a district takes on the proprietary role; and, without taking on this role, it would be impossible to have a school. Factors such as decreasing/increasing student populations, disasters, the selling of district land, the purchasing of land for the district, and/or leasing/renting facilities to community groups will always be part of the business of schooling.

When leasing out facilities, it is important that a district policy on facilities usage be in place and up-to-date. A policy also has to be in place for the use of school buses by outside groups. Today, it is imperative that the school district share its facilities with the community. In the age of accountability, district officials have to be wise stewards of the public's monies.

REFLECTION QUESTIONS

1. What are your current policies relating to facility use? Are they up-to-date, amended, or does the district need a policy?
2. Are these adequate to ensure that you keep sovereign immunity?
3. What possible changes do you as a district need to make?
4. Are you guarding against exceptions for certain individuals to the district policies that could compromise the district's nonproprietary role later on?
5. What are your current policies relating to transportation usage?
6. Develop a professional-development training for the board and administrators that demonstrates that the district values student education over proprietary revenues. This will at the least include how to live the mission statement, communication, and perception.

Chapter Nine

School-Bond Elections

Running a bond election: How successful were you in getting it to pass? How did you do that?

Passing a school-bond election is essential for the physical continuance of education. The *physical continuance* consists of the buildings, grounds, school buses, technology, and other items needed to provide a quality education for students. Many districts have old buildings that are in need of repair or replacement. Remember, if it is too expensive to remodel or not feasible, then a bond issue needs to be passed.

CASE STUDY

Union Public Schools (UPS) has a history of passing bond issues. One example is when they passed a bond issue for $21.6 million, which was for the Union Collegiate Academy (UCA; $16,275,000) and other items. These other items, which were add-ons, were textbooks, computers, school site allocations, uniforms, hardware, security equipment, roofing, and contingency/ bond fees.

In the case study, the district did not need new buildings but was asking the voters to approve addition onto an existing building because of district reconfiguration. It was the superintendent's job to convince the public, which also means the board of education, that the addition was needed and warranted. This took time coupled with explanations, as passing a bond issue means that taxes will go up.

UPS had 15,010 students in nineteen school sites, which was a very small increase in enrollment over 2009–2010. UPS is located within the city limits of Tulsa and Broken Arrow. The bond issue was promoted as a need to make space for tenth graders to "enroll concurrently in high school and Tulsa community college or Tulsa Technology Center" (Archer & Eger 2011).

Archer and Eger (2011) go on to say that the other monies were to be used to build a ninth-grade center, which wasn't mentioned in the additional items. UPS currently has an intermediate high school, which houses ninth- and tenth-grade students. It was also promoted as the second phase of the UCA. In 2010, the voters had approved the first phase of UCA for $12 million. The total cost of this new addition to a stable-grow school district, counting first and second stages, is $33.6 million.

The UPS Web site about the proposition listed the following as what the bond issue would pay for:

- Union Collegiate Academy (UCA) Wing $16,275,000
- Textbooks, media books, software, program subscriptions 1,092,600
- Computers, printers, computer lab upgrades 763,300
- School site allocations 570,000
- Uniforms, equipment, and technology for Fine Arts, Athletics and Spirit, instruments for Band and Orchestra 365,000
- Hardware, software subscriptions, maintenance agreements, equipment, fencing, security equipment, parking, sidewalks, playgrounds, dumpsters, carpet and flooring, and boilers, roofing, track replacement, pole vault pit cover, cooling tower 1,784,100
- Contingency and bond fees 750,000

To pass this bond issue, UPS administrators started to campaign about a year in advance. The following were frequently asked questions and the answers that were given:

Q. Why is passage of this bond proposition important to Union?
A. The district's general fund is for salaries, utilities, and other recurring operating expenses. It is through the issuance of bonds that Union is able to pay for capital expenditures such as buildings (construction), textbooks, instructional technology, and equipment. Without bond propositions, the district would have to tap into its general fund to pay for the facilities and instructional tools our children need, leaving little money to hire teachers or conduct daily operations.
Q. How will passage of this bond proposition affect my taxes?
A. The district pays off existing bonds and its property base continues to grow, therefore that portion of estimated ad valorem tax attributed to Union Public Schools will be maintained at its traditional level.
Q. Why is my vote important?

A. Contrary to most elections, state law requires school bond propositions to pass by a 60 percent super majority. This makes each vote critical.

Q. Where do I vote?

A. Vote at your regular polling place used in country, state, and national elections.

In addition to these questions and answers, the superintendent of schools wrote a letter (see table 9.1) to the patrons of the district ("Message to Voters" 2011).

The week of the election there was a major snowstorm in the Tulsa area, and because of snow-packed neighborhoods, all of the election sites (28) were combined into one election site at the Union basketball arena. A total of 2,239 out of the 77,413 population voted which is 2.9 percent. Usually 2 to 6 percent of the voters turn out to vote. The superintendent of UPS was pleased with the turnout (Archer 2011).

Not all patrons and community members living within the Union Public School district were as happy with this bond issue. Some comments expressed disgust, concern about taxes, and accusations of wasting taxpayer money.

- Was this bond issue needed, or was this just district administrators desiring something different, reconfiguration?
- Will student scores increase?
- Have AP opportunities been offered to tenth-graders in the current configuration?
- What will we do with the additional space at the intermediate high school when the tenth-graders leave?
- Is this a necessary burden to put on our taxpayers during a time of fiscal uncertainty?
- Is this the right time to run a bond-issue election—when our state is in fiscal distress?
- How do we ethically back this proposal to our patrons?

These are some questions you have to ask and answer. Then you'll have to make the call and live with your conscience.

There are several steps in passing a bond issue, and the superintendent in the case study followed these steps. Scholastic.com ("Ten Steps to Pass a Bond Issue" 2011) recommends the following *ten steps* for passing a bond issue:

Table 9.1. Superintendent letter to patrons

Dear Union Patrons:

Building on resounding voter support last year, the second phase of the Union High School Collegiate Academy (UCA) is the center point of the February 8, 2011 bond issue. This new wing of the High School will usher in a new day for students in Union by transforming educational opportunities during the high school years. Added space at the High School will provide room for 10th graders to join High School campus life. The current Intermediate High School building will become a Ninth Grade Center following the structure of Union's other Grade Centers from sixth to eighth grade. Since district goals focus on ensuring that all students are college and career ready when they graduate from high school, this new configuration will support all aspects of college and career preparation. The Ninth Grade Center students will focus on building a plan for High School graduation and career awareness. Opportunities for Advanced Placement (AP) and concurrent enrollment will begin at 10th grade, allowing students to earn both high school and college credit simultaneously. Classes at Tulsa Technology Center will continue to be available to juniors and seniors, and it will also be possible to take both Union High School and concurrent college courses "virtually" (online) in the near future.

Most students at Union have traditionally headed for college upon graduation, but we can help them be even more prepared. This new structure will assist both students and parents to have a seamless transition between high school and college while saving time and more since concurrent and AP enrollment at Union can save parents thousands of dollars in college tuition.

In addition to the new Union High School Collegiate Academy win, the 2011 bond issue deals with immediate capital needs throughout the district that will affect each and every student. Textbooks, library books, technology, and major replacements such as cooling towers, roofs, carpet and tile—all absolutely critical—complete the $21.6 million request for voter approval.

The UCA wing and other big projects such as roof replacements are being completed in phases to ensure that taxes do not rise. Since 60 percent of voter approval is necessary to pass a bond issue, it is critical for all Union patrons to understand the importance of their individual February 8 vote. All the items that will be completed by the 2011 bond are included in our publication, *The Communicator*, and online.

In our ever-changing world, Union strives to be ahead of the curve providing maximum support and opportunities for all of our students to be successful. Our outstanding facilities, caring faculty/staff, and comprehensive instructional programs contribute to our reputation as a premiere school district, which then leads to community pride and strong property values for all homeowners in the Union School District. Patron support of bond issues has been consistently positive and is instrumental in keeping us ahead of the curve.

Thank you for your support,
Dr. [Superintendent]
P.S. $21.6–Million Bond Passage Will NOT Increase Taxes

"Message to Voters" (2011)

1. *Personalize your pitch.* Keep the flow of communication going, and always look for ways to connect with community members on a personal level. Find out how various groups will react to specific features in the bond issue—well in advance of elections day.

2. *Establish financial credibility.* Emphasize the district's sound financial judgment as often as possible. Release your annual financial audit to the public and make school officials available to answer questions. If your community doesn't trust you to handle money, they're not going to hand you a check.

3. *Give voters clear information.* Tell community residents where the money will go and what the needs are. Avoid too many specifics, which will likely change before the money arrives. Nothing sinks a bond faster than squabbling over minutiae.

4. *Think through your budget carefully.* Don't pare down a number just to get a bond passed that won't meet your needs. Going back to the well too often sounds alarms about financial planning.

5. *Decide who gets what.* Delineate how and when each school will get a piece of the pie. There is nothing worse than rivalry among schools when trying to pass a big-figure bond.

6. *Be apolitical.* Avoid giving any perception that the bond issue is aligned with political battles on the school board or in the administration, otherwise voters will turn the polls into a referendum on the political feud, rather than on the bond.

7. *Consider the timing.* Some states mandate the timing of bond votes. If that's not the case in your state, think hard about the best time of year to bring out voters who'll support your cause.

8. *Remember the childless voters.* To win an election, you need to convince voters without school-age children to support school spending.

9. *Accountability is key.* Voters will hold you accountable for tying student performance to expenditures, for judicious funding of your project, and for reporting back to the public about how finances were disbursed.

10. *Think creatively.* Take advantage of the political climate by typing the bond to the issues that community members are most concerned about.

DeJONG (2007) lists the *top ten trends* in school-facility planning. These are:

1. *Declining enrollment.*

2. *Life beyond No Child Left Behind.* As we move into the future we will realize that our country's competitive edge in a global economy is creativity and innovation, which are derived, in part, from the arts.

3. *Any place, any time learning.* Students have always learned outside of school buildings, and new technological possibilities will challenge traditional facilities even further.

4. *Flexible buildings.* School facility designs must allow for pedagogical changes, which means the concept of flexible buildings is moving to totally new definitions.

5. *Global focus.* Jobs that have gone off-shore are not coming back. Will the United States still be the center of the universe?

6. *Modernizing democracy.* A wide variety of independent school boards and/or committees are being considered as more schools become thematic or charter-based. Facility planning is becoming increasingly transparent as a result of new technologies and increased access to data.

7. *Green buildings/sustainability.* Green buildings are on the radar screen. Future schools design will incorporate energy efficiency and a greater concern about the environment. New laws and standards are on the horizon too.

8. *Geographical Information Systems (GIS).* GIS has evolved as the new software standard for facility planning and management. It provides new ways to visually display complex data so it is more understandable.

9. *Safety and security.* The tragedy at Virginia Tech reminds us how vitally important safety and security are. The way a building is laid out or how the program is organized have the biggest impact on safety and security. This is far more important than active security systems like motion detectors or surveillance cameras.

10. *Renovations, modernizations, and replacements.* School buildings built in the 1950s and 60s during the post WWII baby boom era are aging. Unfortunately these were not our finest buildings. The process has begun to fully modernize or replace these facilities. This will continue for the next fifteen plus years.

Hill (2005) lists a ten-point checklist for educational excellence. He states:

An educational facility master plan is about educational *excellence*. Planning for the future! Quality learning! Practicality and efficiency! These major educational objectives must be properly accommodated within a well built and well maintained learning environment. Simply stated, "sticks and bricks" by themselves don't sell well to the public.

Any comprehensive facility master plan must put the *"life"* into "lifelong learning." It must make buildings personal and about children. And then, it must translate that personal touch into a practical, realistic, and cost-effective solution for building remodeling and new construction.

Hill's (2005) ten points are the following:

1. Plan "Futuristically" and Practically for Remodeling and New Construction. It is always more fun to plan a new building. People seem to think they can get off to a fresh start and try new ideas. A clean new site seems like the perfect situation to reinvent learning, etc., etc., etc. Remember, 90% of the "schools of the future" are already built. They should, however, be remodeled for new curriculum trends and future flexibility! Consideration! Proper planning of a remodeled facility is as important as planning for new construction. And, remodeling can often accomplish 90% or more of the new instructional concepts, technology uses, and maintenance efficiencies associated with a new building. Remodeling projects can and must be used as an opportunity to reinvent staff thinking about educational delivery, technology uses, team activities, and more.

2. Consider Future Trends Appropriate for Your District—Do's and Don'ts. An important aspect of any facility planning process is to consider adopting appropriate educational trends. Sometimes this is done by bringing in an outside expert who explains to the district that they are "far behind other districts" and proceeds to chastise the educators accordingly as being "out of date." This approach never works! You can "teach an old dog new tricks." And this does apply to educators and administrators. However, successfully adopting new ideas begins with thoroughly understanding and appreciating what the district is already doing well and building upon those accomplishments—one individual at a time. More often than might be expected, many staff members are already doing great deeds. Others want to implement new ideas but are often unable to do so because of the facilities, limited funding, or fear of embarrassing colleagues. A planning process that properly acknowledges and builds upon existing visions and accomplishments already in place can create a climate for embracing even more appropriate new ideas during and after the remodeling or new construction program. Consideration! The facility planning process must be founded on a thorough understanding of the district's current practices and visions and then aligning future trend opportunities in a context of "acceptance and praise," not chastisement and shame.

3. Projects are NEVER Too Small to Plan—except if you have a small amount of money to waste. A small school district once suggested that a project was too small to afford planning. They thought, "Just Do IT!" This approach may work for Nike. But be assured, Nike plans their least expensive shoe very carefully. Even a few hours of oversight on a small project by a properly trained educational planning professional should improve efficiency, offer options for instructional enhancement, and often times, save money. Advanced planning should help:

- Define program goals.
- Reach clarity about how students, staff, public, etc. will be better served, how learning issues should be accomplished, and how many students will be affected.
- Outline the complete extent of technologies to be used... not just computers.

With today's internet technologies, such a small-project review can be conducted using digitized photos and floor plans, combined with conversations by telephone with educational leaders. In a recent example, two Texas high school general classrooms proposed for conversion to special education were substantially enhanced by a variety of recommendations which addressed lighting, color, visual connectivity through interior windows, exterior tinted windows to reduce glare, directional speakers, appropriately located instructional television, and even relocating an old HVAC unit to increase storage area efficiency. The money would have been spent on something anyway, but by properly combining multiple elements of functionality in a more unified fashion, the solution was ultimately less expensive, while substantially improving educational delivery. The process also assured the educators that their ideas were on target. In the end, they had an expanded sense of educational clarity and operational efficiency. Consideration! Educationally plan ALL projects—big and small. But, make sure that any expenditure for planning makes sense in light of the expected project value.

4. Net-to-Gross Ratios can be really "Gross" ... if planned poorly... and great when planned well. An often totally overlooked aspect of educational facility design is the net-to-gross ratio. This is the percentage of space allocated to hallways, walls, mechanical rooms, and other areas to support the "net" usable academic spaces, which consist of the interior dimensions of classrooms, libraries, etc. All too often, a hidden and less obvious factor escalating total construction costs is the amount of area that may be unknowingly assigned to "gross" square

footage. Ironically, school facilities with very high net-to-gross ratios may not make wonderful schools, as small corridors may make circulation difficult. Additionally, many of our wonderful schools of the past conveyed the importance of education by generously allocating space for public assembly and circulation, but at what cost?. The planning intention is informed financial analysis and informed decision-making regarding this important net-to-gross design element. Any master-planning situation should have a clear, up-front objective of clarity on the gross square footage assigned to any new or remodeled building solution. Approaches may include:

- Planning for the most efficient design standards as starting position.
- Then, assign specific area to those "dignifying" spaces proposed for a commons, main entry, team areas, just as if they are educational programmed spaces.
- Then, at a macro scale, make informed decisions as to the total gross square foot cost compared to the affordable project budget. Further, at the micro design level;
- Analyze unusually shaped rooms, such as triangles, that often create wasted corners that never get efficient educational use. Odd shapes, which look "cool" in plan, can reduce the efficiency and use of interior classroom space by as much as 20 percent or more.
- Science labs with a huge demonstration table and teacher "sage on the stage" design can also result in as much as 200 square feet lost from educational use.

In summary, avoid accepting an overall average net-to-gross ratio for the whole building. Rather, separately analyze areas, such as gymnasiums, which are very large and thus have very efficient net-to-gross ratios compared to classrooms, technology education areas, offices, etc. Then, factor in and agree on the extent of "special" spaces to make the building "timeless" and an asset to the community as part of a total objective, and quantifiable value engineering analysis process. Consideration! If the project is over budget and square footage reductions are necessary, look at the gross square footage utilizing a systematic and objective process.

5. Room Dimensions Really Count—length and width of rooms are NOT arbitrary to learning results. Proper building design is an extensive three-phase process. Oftentimes educators are only involved in Phase I design (Schematics), which accounts for all the rooms and basically locates them in the building. Square footage size is also defined during schematic design. Factors that really make the space work for students, teachers, and learning, are identified in Phase II

design (Design Development) when actual room layouts are finalized. This is where the "rubber" often hits the road. Consideration! It is essential that serious attention be given by educators to Phase II interior room designs and dimensions of spaces in addition to Phase I conceptual schematic designs.

6. Plan Review—A Third-Party Critique can save Money and Improve Efficiency. Many districts are having an outside third party (educational planner) review and critique schematic and design development documents. Such a review can either confirm programmatic functionality or suggest modifications to the design to better accomplish educational objectives cost affectively. Often times the design team and participating educators can get "too close" to the proposed solution and thus overlook issues of net-to-gross ratio, room dimensions, and functional orientations important to learning. Consideration! An outside critique and plan review by an educational planner can be accomplished in a day or two and offer numerous alternatives to improve efficiency, long-term flexibility, and possible reduce project cost.

7. Building Capacity—The Hidden Secret to Efficiency and Referendum Success. Properly portraying building utilization and capacity is an important tool by which a district can promote building efficiency to the community and increase the likelihood of passing a bond referendum. Yet, understanding utilization and capacity and translating it clearly to the public can be a difficult task. All too often capacity is associated with an overall average building utilization factor such as 70-80 percent. If there are 1,000 student stations, (locations for students to sit), an 80 percent utilization would mean the school would best serve an 800-student enrollment capacity. Yet, in reality, the efficiency of utilization may fluctuate greatly from department to department. This is particularly true for high schools, where efficient utilization planning may try to increase capacity of expensive and large science rooms, art rooms, and physical education areas. It may be preferable to operate classrooms at a slightly reduced efficiency and in a fashion that will allow effective teaming, schools within school organizations. These popular emerging operations focus on an expended integration of core curriculum instruction. Consideration! Think of capacity and efficiency on an area-by-area basis and not necessarily summarize this feature building wide. This will improve operational presentation, economize on building size/cost, and be more understandable and acceptable to the community—resulting in both efficiency and educational excellence.

8. A Good Master Plan DOES Include Maintenance. Building maintenance, renovation, and education should be inextricably intertwined. These are the features of a quality capital resource master plan. Impor-

tant emphasis must certainly be placed on the fundamentals of physical conditions such as roofs, mechanical systems, window efficiency, plumbing, and other maintenance items. Unfortunately, a division between maintenance and educational facilities arises when these two departments are treated separately within the organizational structure. Allowing maintenance repairs to overshadow educational objectives may prove dysfunctional for both education and maintenance. First, it can result in extensive spending on maintenance items to such an extent that upfront cost for repairs overshadow truly needed educational requirements. Alternatively, properly planning the educational requirements first and then, phasing maintenance over time can address both the up front learning concerns of parents, i.e., educational excellence, while also allowing the phased expenditure of maintenance items. A successful master plan will integrate the best long-term replacement/depreciation schedule of maintenance needs with curriculum changes suggested by educational future trends. Consideration! A brand spanking newly remodeled building founded on yesterday's educational methods and technologies will not sell well to today's more sophisticated parental community.

9. Partnerships in Planning—business, government, civic groups, community colleges. Increasingly, facility master plans are incorporating outside local groups in a variety of mutually beneficial partnership arrangements. This can include a variety of options, such as students departing the campus for community college level on-the-job training, or allowing community colleges onto school sites to demonstrate advancements in technology, curricula, and career opportunities. A more recent facility trend is the "Learning Atrium" where businesses have a defined multi-use space where they can set up equipment in a safe and secure manner and make business presentations to students and staff alike. In the best models, business applications are planned and scheduled with high school educators to correspond to the school's multi-disciplinary teams who can then align classroom instruction in terms of practical and authentic career applications. Consideration! Promote educational excellence and the facility master plan to community colleges and small successful businesses for possible grant funding, shared space use, and enhanced public support.

10. Create a Bond Referendum Package Beneficial to the Entire Community In the end, a facility master plan must resonate with all members the community to win at election time. For the parents, it must demonstrate educational excellence in a practical, efficient, and safe manner. For senior citizens, it must show that their real estate investment will be protected and even be enhanced through the provision of a quality educational system functioning in well-maintained and pleasant look-

ing facilities. Businesses must feel that the enhanced educational solutions will produce a more stable workforce and career path for students who may go directly from school to work or onto local community colleges. Consideration! Create and promote a facility master plan
that serves the whole community, not just the students, staff, and
administration. A facility master plan cannot simply be "sticks and
bricks", charts and graphs, spreadsheets and dollar totals. It cannot
read like the annual report for a widget manufacturing company. A
successful facility master plan must focus on educational excellence to
win at the ballot box. It must give "life" to "lifelong learning" and
connect on a personal with the entire community. And, it must be
within budget and practical. Is this all possible?. . .with the right
planning process, more often than might be expected

—Permission to reprint granted by Franklin Hill of Franklin Hill
and Associates

If a new superintendent is fortunate enough to begin his or her tenure in a
district that is already prepared to move forward, the acquisition of new real
property can go easily. That's a big *if.* Said one fortunate soul in Arkansas,
"We have purchased fifty-three acres since I have taken over for future
development. Probably paid a little too much for some of the property but in
the end it worked out great for the district. There were some eminent domain
issues before I took over with the family [who owned the land that was
needed by the district] and this helped ease the ill feelings."

Referencing the "First Significant Legal Challenge" topic of the next
chapter, this superintendent said:

> The first significant legal challenge was getting the district out of the eminent
> domain issue. The former superintendent was not very well liked by the family
> and they pretty much refused to deal with him. He was right the whole time
> but they would never concede to that. Fortunately when I took over they were
> more open-minded towards a fair settlement for both parties. Legal counsel
> will nearly always do what you want but will straddle the fence when answer-
> ing your questions.

CHECKLISTS FOR PLANNING AND PASSING A BOND ISSUE

A. *Develop a long-range plan*
__ Make an enrollment projection.
__ Conduct a school-building survey.
__ Adopt a long-range building plan.

__ Take official action.
__ Enlist citizen participation.
B. *Generate public support*
__ Assess public attitude.
__ Develop a strategy for gaining public support.
__ Establish a citizen advisory committee.
__ Consider the use of the installment plan.
__ Start the public information plan early.
__ Organize coffee groups or other small groups.
__ Develop a greater awareness of public opinion.
__ Become thoroughly familiar with every detail on the proposed building.
__ Know the real issue underlying the opposition's point of view.
C. *Plan the school building*
__ Obtain planning funds.
__ Secure professional services.
__ Select the school site.
__ Prepare a comprehensive set of educational specifications.
__ Stage 1: Preliminary drawings—schematic design phase.
__ Stage 2: Progress prints—design development plan.
__ Stage 3: Final working drawings and specifications.
__ Stage 4: Procedures after the approval of drawings and specifications.
D. *Prepare the public for the bond issue and its successful passage*
Question and Answer Bond Election Information needs to be completed and provided to all of the patrons in the school district.

SUMMARY

Passing a school-bond election is essential for the physical continuance of education. The physical continuance consists of the buildings, grounds, school buses, technology, and other items needed to provide a quality education for students.

Ten steps to passing a bond issue from Scholastic.com ("Ten Steps to Pass a Bond Issue" 2011) are "personalize the pitch"; "establish financial credibility"; "give clear information"; "think through your budget"; "decide who gets what"; "be apolitical"; "consider the timing"; "remember all voters"; "the key is accountability"; and "be creative."

Hill's (2005) ten points are "plan 'futuristically' and practically"; "consider future trends appropriate for your district"; "projects are never too small to plan"; "net-to-gross ratios can be really 'gross'"; "room dimensions really count"; "plan review"; "build capacity"; "a good master plan does include maintenance"; "partnerships in planning"; and "create a bond referendum package beneficial to the entire community."

REFLECTION QUESTIONS

1. Why is a bond election needed at this time? What amount is needed?
2. What is the date for the bond election?
3. How will this amount affect the community's property taxes?
4. What is the tax impact on the homeowner sixty-five or older?
5. How will the students benefit from the bond program? How will the bond program improve education in our town?
6. Which schools will benefit from this proposed bond program?
7. What is the schedule for projects?
8. With the booming (stable, shrinking) construction market in our community, how accurate are the estimates?
9. How does the district fund ongoing maintenance and renovation projects?
10. What factors will decide where the *undesignated* school in Proposition 1 (or whatever fits your bond election) will be located?
11. Which schools have enrollments above their permanent capacity, and where are they located?
12. What are the growth trends in the district?
13. How was the scope of proposed bond work developed?
14. How will the independent school district ensure that the money is spent appropriately?
15. How will the proposed technology improvements (or other improvements, depending on your bond) be allocated to the individual campuses?
16. Why are we renovating schools rather than replacing them?
17. Why is the district building new schools when the total enrollment of the district has increased only slightly in the past five years?
18. How many portables are currently being utilized in the district?
19. What percentage of the current school population is served in portables?
20. What is the advantage of refinancing contractual obligations?
21. What funding is provided in the bond program to address functional-equity improvements?

Chapter Ten

First Significant Legal Challenge

First significant legal challenge: How effective was your legal counsel in working with you and your board? How did you know that a situation that was brought to you was one that would need legal advice?

A superintendent serves as the district's curriculum, fiscal, and community leader. Superintendents are the CEOs of their districts. They are responsible for ensuring that the school district carries out all of the laws and policies relating to the district in its state. The district's legal counsel has the primary responsibility for advising the superintendent and school-district personnel on legal, employee-contract, administration, and personnel matters.

The board of education sets policy not otherwise controlled by state and federal laws. Regulations, set by the superintendent, define the procedures by which board policy is carried out within the school district. The policies and regulations are continually revised and amended to comply with current state and federal laws. Sometimes a district might become lax in this area, in which case there would be many outdated policies in the district's policy book. Policies and regulations can be changed without notice, and the board of education reserves the right to enforce changes immediately.

Larger districts will have an office of general counsel. This office is responsible for providing proactive legal advice to the school board, superintendent, and school district on all legal matters relating to the operation of the district, and for representing the school board and superintendent in legal and administrative proceedings. The general counsel also advises the school board at all school-board meetings. Henderson (2003) explains that complex issues in the educational environment often requires legal counsel. Effective representation assists the district in controlling legal issues that could burden the operation of the district.

Valente (1994) states, "The law controls what schools should do, who should do it, and how it should be done" (3). Legally recognized interests in education come from the state, the federal government, parents, students, teachers, and others. Public education is the responsibility of the individual states. The Tenth Amendment gives unspecified powers to the states, and therefore state constitutions direct their legislatures to provide for a state public-education system.

Rice v. Commonwealth and *Epperson v. Arkansas* are two milestone court cases that confirmed that education rests with the states where federal interests are not implicated (Valente 1994). The federal interest deals with civil liberties (i.e., freedom of speech, press, association, and religion, and immunities from discrimination) and curriculum (e.g., national security, economic welfare).

Parents hold constitutionally protected rights to control the upbringing of their children. An issue here is how you balance the interests of the parents when they are in direct opposition to the interests of the government, teaching professionals, or the general citizenry (Valente 1994).

Student-interest litigation has increased dramatically since the 1960s. Valente (1994) says that the "rights of students range from education-centered issues to civil rights, such as freedom of speech, religion, and privacy" (5). Issues that have arisen in the twenty-first century are illegal immigration, cell-phone usage/texting, Internet bullying, and so forth. Teachers, school employees, taxpayers, and various officials also have a legally recognized interest.

Lawsuits can arise from a variety of places: the *school environment* (school safety, commercialism in schools, school facilities); *constitutional issues* (religion in the public school, free speech and expression); *students* (Internet use, student organizations and clubs, part-time admission of students, student medicine, student records, bullying, illegal immigrants); *personnel* (evaluation, governmental immunity, contracts); and *accountability* (malpractice).

When a person becomes dissatisfied or angry, a lawsuit can arise. Because educational institutions are people institutions, they are susceptible to lawsuits at both the federal and state level. LaMance (2009) identifies the following as common types of lawsuits against schools:

- **Discrimination**. A school can generally be sued for discriminating in its employment practices or with regard to admitted students.
- **Excessive and severe punishment**. A school can be sometimes be sued for punishing a student. For most lawsuits to be successful, the punishment must be severe. Severe punishments are generally those that can, or are known to cause death, great bodily harm, dismemberment, disfigurement, or extreme pain.

- **Sexual misconduct**. Schools are usually liable for any sexual misconduct of a teacher to a student. Title IX of the *Educational Amendment Act of 1972* also can make a school liable for the sexual misconduct of a student to another student. Sexual misconduct can include sexual harassment, molestation, sexual assault, or rape.
- **Failure to supervise**. Because a school has a semi-custodial relationship with it students, a school can be liable for the acts of a student. Generally, a school must act negligently in supervising a student who then commits a crime or injures another person to be liable.
- **Improper discharge of a teacher or any employee**. Teachers who have been improperly discharged on the grounds of incompetency or immoral and/or criminal conduct can sometimes sue the school that fired them. Such teachers generally have to exhaust all administrative remedies before they can sue the school. . . .
- **Educational malpractice**. If a school fails to adequately educate a student in basic academic skills, it is sometimes possible for that student to sue the school.

As you can see, a school can be sued for a variety of reasons. The key to not getting sued is to do what a reasonably prudent person would do. If you do get sued, make certain that you have your list of evidence and documentation. In regards to educational malpractice, as of date no student has won a case.

Any person or group can sue a school. The most common defendants are school boards, school districts, individual schools, teachers, principals, and superintendents. In lawsuits against the school board, the superintendent is usually named, as is the teacher, principal, or coach.

The context in which we are speaking in this chapter is that of a civil, not criminal, lawsuit. Civil lawsuits are not usually about jail time or fines. Civil lawsuits are usually about restitution or getting someone to stop doing something.

Wasser (2009) recommends the following ten steps for minimizing litigation against your district:

- Hire an attorney on retainer to be present at all board meetings and be available for questions as they arise.
- Encourage a united front among board members and the superintendent.
- Ensure board policies and procedures are in place and up-to-date.
- Incorporate preventive measures into daily practices.
- Familiarize staff, students, parents and community members with school district policies and practices.
- Be clear about expectations of students and staff.

- Be consistent in adhering to policy and procedures.
- Treat people fairly and consistently.
- Always maintain thorough documentation.
- Strengthen communications among board, administration, staff, students, and the community.

In essence, lawsuits can be brought against the school from a number of areas. These are the law governing school studies; religion and public education; professional personnel (legislative control of teacher status); professional personnel (collective bargaining rights); professional personnel (civil rights); student rights and discipline; equal opportunity in public education; federal law remedies for discrimination; tort liability under state law; financing education; and private education (Valente 1994).

HOW DO YOU WIN A LAWSUIT?

Ritchie-Roberts Law Firm (2010) gives the following advice on "How to Win a Lawsuit." When you're getting sued:

1. Don't get emotional and let it show.
2. Having a meltdown or temper tantrum is not beneficial and will be detrimental to your case.
3. Bad new can paralyze you. Resist this.
4. Don't alleviate your stress by developing a bad habit.
5. Today's headlines is tomorrow's "fish wrap."

Be calm because it will be perceived by you that the world is coming to an end and is out of control but stay focused and do the following:

1. Don't let your rage be displayed if front of people on the news who could be your jurors.
2. Never ever call the other party.
3. You can "catch more flies with honey than with vinegar" Treat people like you'd like to be treated.

Do you want to win your lawsuit? This involves professional collegial communications between the plaintiff's attorney and defendant's attorney as to:

1. Procedures and protocol that each party will abide by.
2. Clearly stating the facts.
3. Clearly stating and knowing the law.
4. Have a convincing argument so the judge or arbitrator sides with you.

The first thing you need to do is to make certain that you have all of your materials and documents in order. Next, you have to learn about the type of lawsuit and what the plaintiff is seeking? A lawsuit is an action brought by a plaintiff seeking remedies. These might include:

1. Setting an injunction.
2. Getting a declaration to stop future legal action.
3. Collecting money, punitive damages, and interest.

Gather the facts and get them organized. All of the facts needed to be assembled in a very timely manner. The following is needed:

1. Identifying and knowing the witnesses for each side.
2. Identifying who made the mistake or did the wrong.
3. All documents concerning the dispute are in order and collected

—Reprint permission granted by Ritchie-Roberts Law Firm

After you've gathered this information, use it to put together a detailed chronological and narrative statement of the facts. From this develop a flow chart of what took place.

If you are caught in *arbitration*, which is a legal method for the resolution of disputes outside the courts, there will be two types of arbitration: mandatory and nonmandatory. If you are in *mediation*, which is a form of resolution, the goal is to assist two or more disputants in to reaching an agreement. Usually, all parties must view the mediator as impartial. If you are in *litigation*, which is when a lawsuit is brought before a court and the plaintiff is seeking a legal remedy, judgment may be in the form of court orders, penalties, damages, injunctions, or declaratory judgment.

A lawsuit is started by the complaint. Then follows a flurry of motions, then an answer, then discovery, and finally trial. In an interview, Ryan Roberts (2011), of the Richey and Roberts law firm, identified the following as the "anatomy of a lawsuit":

1. **Complaint/Petition**—States all causes of actions plus all necessary facts to show that a cause of action exists and the Plaintiff is a proper plaintiff.
2. **Flurry of Motions**—Motion to dismiss, to strike, or to require a more definite *statement of the complaint*. (These are rarely granted and many times this step is bypassed.)
3. **Answer**—Answers complaint one allegation at a time, separately admitting or denying each allegation.

4. **Discovery**—Request for admission, request for production, interrogatories, depositions, Subpoenas and providing witness and exhibit lists to opposing parties.
5. **Motion Work**—Motions for Summary Judgment, Motions in Limine, Motion to Compel Discovery.
6. **Trial**—Formal presentation of facts and law for determination of a winner pursuant to *Rules of Evidence*.

Roberts (2011) goes on to say that he believes the reason most lawsuits are lost is because of the lack of evidence. "You can't make up what is not there."

The standard practice per Roberts of The Ritchie-Roberts Law Firm (2011) used to win any type of lawsuit are as follows:

a) Procedure. Be familiar with Civil Rules of Procedure and Local Court Rules so that "technicalities" do not derail your position.
b) Facts. It is important to emphasize those facts which best support your position.
c) Substantive Law. You will want to locate any statutes, cases, rules that support your position. If you have a poor set of facts, substantive law will be your only chance at success.

A lawsuit begins with a filing of a complaint or petition with the court. This is the first of the pleadings that are filed. The clerk of the court then issues a summons for service of process upon the defendants. As a defendant you must respond by:

- Motion to strike
- An answer
- A motion to dismiss
- A cross complaint/counter claim

NOTE—A lawsuit can be won in this phase.

The next phase is the Judicial Management Conferences or scheduling conferences. During this time the judge will hear from each party, their counsel, and set dates and decide on:

- Dates for discovery to be completed
- Dates that a settlement conference must be performed by
- Dates for exchange of witnesses and exhibits
- Resolution of discovery disputes
- Case summary by the attorneys
- Date of the pre-trial conference
- Trial date

The *burden of proof* is convincing the judge or jury that your version of the facts is the truthful and correct version. In a civil case you have to convince the judge or jury by a *preponderance of the evidence*, which is 51 percent or more that your version of the facts is true.

A lawsuit can be won in *discovery phase* by the party not providing proper documents. *Discovery* is the time you question your opponent's version of the facts. The defendant can do the following to help them win a case in this phase:

- Make a motion to compel the discovery.
- Request sanctions against the plaintiff for not responding.
- Terminal sanctions striking the plaintiff's pleading because they didn't cooperate.
- Make a Motion to Limine to preclude this evidence from being presented at trial.

Types of discovery are:

- Interrogatories
- Request for production of documents
- Request for admissions
- Depositions
- Third party subpoenas

Expert testimony: You can win your case before going to trial. This is done in the following ways:

- Default judgment
- Motion for summary judgment
- Motion to dismiss
- Involuntary dismissal by the court
- Voluntary dismissal
- Settlement

If you end up going to trial, there are two types of trial, judge trial or jury trial. During the trial each party can make motions for various legal and factual theories, such as:

- Motion to directed verdict
- Motion for non-suit
- Motion to dismiss

- Motion for summary judgment
- Motion in limine

After a judgment is rendered, the defense can make motions for various issues while the plaintiff can make motions for other issues such as attorney fees. After a final decision is made, either party may appeal the judgment if they are unhappy with the verdict and the jurisdiction grants their ability to appeal.

In summary, winning a lawsuit involves:

- organization
- education
- presenting the facts, law, and procedure in the clearest way
- keeping a good attitude.

Pauline Sampson (2011), a former superintendent and current university professor, says, "Developing relationships, documentations, and following the letter of the law will keep you out of court. Money plays a big role in whether you want to fight the lawsuit or settle out of court." She goes on to say that you always need to do what is right even though a board might not want to fight a case because of finances.

She reflected on a time when she had all of the documentation and was ready to go forward, but the case would have cost in the neighborhood of $25,000 to fight, her district was in financial trouble, and so the board opted not to go forward. That one really frustrated her because what the board did was not best for the system.

Dr. Roberts reflects:

> When I became superintendent at my last position, the district was just on the final stages of finishing up a lawsuit brought against them, *Eyvine Hearn, United States of America v. Muskogee Public School District 020* (C.A. No: CIV 03-598-S). The Rutherford Institute sued the district on behalf of the plaintiff 's father, who was of the Islamic faith. The Rutherford Institute was joined by the Justice Department of the United States. They challenged the validity of the Muskogee Public School District's dress code, which prohibited her from wearing her holy scarf, or *hijab*, within the district's buildings.
>
> The United States intervened under Title IX of the Civil Rights Act of 1974. The plaintiffs and the United States contended that the plaintiff's constitutional rights had been violated and were also violated according to Oklahoma law.
>
> The defendant, Muskogee School District, contended that the dress code was consistent with the guidelines on religious expression in public schools that were published by the United States Department of Education in 1998 (see appendix B). To avoid the costly litigation, that district agreed to resolve the claims. The district could not afford to fight this as they already faced obligations to the State of Oklahoma for over $2 million.

To settle this lawsuit, the parties agreed to the scope and duration of the consent order:

1. Remain in effect for six years.
2. Court shall retain jurisdiction during this six-year period to ensure compliance.
3. The parties, in good faith, will resolve informally any differences regarding the interpretation of this Order.
4. The parties agree that time limits may be expanded upon mutual consent of the parties.

The Muskogee School District was required to:

1. Amend the applicable portion of its dress codes.
2. Provide training to all teachers and administrators regarding the amendments to the dress codes.
3. Provide students and parents with copies of the revised dress codes.
4. Certify in writing to the court its compliance with the terms of the order.
5. Permit the plaintiff to wear a *hijab*, effective immediately. The *hijab* was not to cover her face.

The parties reached separate settlement agreements (this was a monetary settlement).

"The ex-superintendent told me," said Dr. Roberts, "that he believed the district was interpreting the law correctly, but the federal government saw it differently." The girl's family sought $80,000 in damages, claiming the dress code discriminated unjustly against religious clothing. The Associated Press (2004) reported that the girl's family was happy the case was over.

Alexander Acosta, assistant U.S. attorney general for civil rights, said, "This settlement reaffirms the principle that public schools cannot require students to check their faith at the schoolhouse door." Acosta went on to say, "It's un-American to fear and to hate." Dr. Roberts concluded, "Finishing off this case was a new learning experience. I learned that just because you feel you are right, you won't necessarily win the case. Many things come into play."

The questions from our study asked, How effective was your legal counsel in working with you and your board? How did you know that a situation that was brought to you was one that would need legal advice? A superintendant in our study with a long résumé of experience reflected:

A couple of cases that came to my attention my first year was when a parent came into my office extremely upset because his son had been sexually bullied by students in the junior high classroom. This was a reverse minority case. The father did not want to sue the district but he wanted action taken.

I had an emergency meeting with the principal and physical education teacher. Upon gathering the facts, I went to the school attorney and presented to him what I had. After much discussion, we decided on moving the teacher to another building and apologized to the parent.

That was a bold step but it was worth the gamble because it would keep our district out of the newspaper and earn support from an irate parent. The parent accepted the apology, we moved the teacher without any threats from the teacher's union, and the guilty students were suspended for the remainder of the year. I knew I would need legal advice the minute I heard the words "sexual harassment."

The second case had to deal with employee harassment by a supervisor. This lady had been working in the technology department and was being harassed by her supervisor. Some of it was very close to sexual harassment. She was keeping a log and had reported the incidents a couple of years earlier to his supervisor but nothing had changed. This time she came to the Personnel Director with these notes and a letter of complaint.

A new superintendent in East Texas reported:

My first legal challenge dealt with a new employee. A week after hiring a coach, he drove to town to meet with the athletes. He was pulled over for speeding and found to have an unusable amount of marijuana in the car. He was not given a ticket or arrested. I found out about the incident from a community member. The employee had already signed a contract by the time I was informed of the situation. Counsel was most helpful in getting a resignation and doing so properly.

Another told us, "We switched legal counsels. The board was not comfortable with the person the old superintendent used."

Another superintendent said:

A teacher hurt a child. I suspended her with pay until it was investigated. Upon completion of the investigation, I brought the issue to the board's attention. The board agreed that legal advice was needed. She was terminated after a hearing. The legal counsel was effective in that the evidence was all presented in a thorough manner. However, it ended up costing the school $75,000 to get the teacher to drop all federal and civil lawsuits.

From another: "Our first real need for legal assistance was as we moved through the RIF process that first year. Clearly, when you are dealing with reduction of personnel, the advice of lawyers is necessary."

Legal challenges come from employees getting in trouble with the law, employees harming a student (physically or verbally), firing an employee, changing protocol (i.e., changing attorneys), reducing staff, and so forth. It seems that most of the time, the situation in which you will need to see the school attorney will pertain either to employees or to students.

According to Dr. Roberts:

> There are many steps to follow. I personally did not hesitate in contacting the attorney for any matter. When giving advice to the board, I could say "on the advice of legal counsel . . . ," and the board readily accepted the recommendation. I've been in two districts where the protocol was to have the school attorney at board meetings. Personally, I did not like that because the board would defer many questions to the attorney.
>
> In one district, the attorney was available at a phone-call's notice. In two other districts in which I worked, the school attorneys were located in other towns and therefore only came to the district when situations demanded it (e.g., closing an elementary school, "riffing" teachers).

LAWSUIT PREVENTION

Patrice McCarthy (2011), chair of the National School Board's Association Council of School Attorneys, suggests the following for preventing school board lawsuits:

1. **Know the boundaries of your authority**. School board authority comes from the state constitution, statutes and administrative regulations. Board policies provide additional direction.
2. **Focus on the board's policy making role**. Boards are policy-making bodies and their role is to determine specific details.
3. **Adhere to the student discipline policy**. Student discipline is an important area in which boards and superintendents should carefully follow the established policies and regulations.
4. **Understand the staff discipline process**. Board members need to understand the procedures that are in place to discipline or fire staff.
5. **Review and adhere to policies on holiday celebrations**. There is a fine line between learning about holiday traditions in school and proselytizing. Court decisions illustrate the challenge of avoiding illegal support of religion, while protecting the First Amendment rights of students.

6. **Be familiar with the laws governing board meetings**. Board members only have power when they act as a body. Individual members do not have the power to make policies or perform official acts unless it is delegated to them by the whole board. The superintendent acts as a representative or agent for the board.

7. **Avoid nepotism and conflicts of interest**. Boards have specific policies addressing the hiring of immediate family members or relatives. States also usually have statutes addressing nepotism. Superintendents also have to be aware of this when hiring their family members.

8. **Understand ethical considerations**. A code of ethics should be adopted that is adhered to by the board, superintendent, and all administrators. Review and discuss the code of ethics annually. The code of ethics should address honesty, fairness, trust, and integrity while supporting high-quality education for all students.

9. **Clarify the roles of board members and the superintendent**. The power of the board can only be exercised when the board meets in a formal meeting. The superintendent is the chief executive officer and has responsibility for daily operations. The board only hires and evaluates the superintendent.

10. **Conduct a thoughtful and thorough superintendent search process**. It is important that boards develop and follow an effective search process. State laws provide some guidance in hiring procedures and certification requirements as well as in Freedom of Information or open meeting laws. (42–43).

Superintendents who adhere to these suggestions will drastically eliminate lawsuits against the board and the superintendent. The publicity around, and timing of, lawsuits are intrusions that are not welcome and can be avoided by following best practices and being alert to and aware of the law and policies.

CHECKLISTS FOR WHEN TO CONTACT THE SCHOOL DISTRICT'S ATTORNEY

A. When (in what situations) should a superintendent call the board's attorney to seek legal advice about a situation concerning both the superintendent and the board?

___ The school attorney is COUNSEL to the district.
___ Egos and self control maintained.
___ Call for an answer to a legal question.

___ Answer what you know, don't bluff.

B. When (in what situations) should a superintendent contact an attorney about his own legal problems with the board?

___ Learn about the issue, and then determine if attorney is needed.
___ Own internal investigation.
___ Position is ethically and morally.
___ A poor evaluation and the board is trying to fire you.
___ Negotiating your contract.

C. At what point should the superintendent have the attorney meet with the board?

___ Worked out with Board of Education in executive session or board workshop.
___ Not a liaison between the board and the attorney.
___ Develop an understanding of new legislations and work as it is published each day to present it to the board.
___ Contact your attorney early.
___An issue perceived in the community as ethical issue, but may not be a legal issue.
___ Take the legal, moral, and ethical high ground.

SUMMARY

Anyone with about one hundred dollars and a lawyer who will listen for twenty minutes can file a lawsuit; doing so takes little talent and even less common sense. All kinds of people file suit. The educational leader who has a high profile (superintendent!) may get sued at some point in his or her professional career. If you do what reasonable and prudent people would do in the same or similar circumstances, the suit may never go to an actual courtroom.

One of the authors, who was recently involved in litigation, was told by his attorney that about 93 percent of cases are settled or abandoned before an actual court appearance. Getting sued is not the end of the world. Do what is ethically and morally right, but keep good relations with the school district's attorney also. Keep good records and make sure your staff does too.

The district's legal counsel has the primary responsibility for advising the superintendent and school district personnel on legal, employee-contract, administration, and personnel matters. LaMance (2009) identifies the following as common lawsuits against schools: "discrimination"; "excessive and severe punishment"; "sexual misconduct"; "failure to supervise"; "improper discharge of a teacher or any employee"; and "educational malpractice."

Wasser (2010) recommends the following ten steps for minimizing litigation against your district: "hire an attorney on retainer to be present at all board meetings and be available for questions as they arise"; "encourage a united front among board members and the superintendent"; "ensure board policies and procedures are in place and up-to-date"; "incorporate preventive measures into daily practices"; "familiarize staff, students, parents and community members with school district policies and practices"; "be clear about expectations of students and staff"; "be consistent in adhering to policy and procedures"; "treat people fairly and consistently"; "always maintain thorough documentation"; and "strengthen communications among board, administration, staff, students, and the community" (4).

When the district is getting sued, keep your calm, inform the board, and visit with the school attorney. The school attorney will require all of the evidence and a list of witnesses. To maximize the district's chance of winning, make certain that all evidence is kept in a secure place and school policies are up-to-date.

REFLECTION QUESTIONS

1. Have I checked to see what the traditional role of the school attorney is in my district? Discuss how you would change the traditional role of the attorney to fit the modern school needs.
2. Have I introduced myself to the school attorney to begin creating a collegial relationship? Discuss the reasons the superintendent needs to have a good relationship with the school attorney.
3. Have I researched former legal challenges that occurred in the district? What were the outcomes? What could have been done differently if the school was not successful in the lawsuit?
4. Are there any current legal challenges occurring in the district? Does the attorney have all of the evidence? What evidence is lacking? Why is it necessary to keep the board informed of legal challenges?
5. Design a board workshop which educates the board about school law and the anatomy of a lawsuit.

Chapter Eleven

First (Annual) Evaluation of Supervisory/Administrative Staff

Your first evaluation of supervisory staff: How accepting were your principals, etc., of your first evaluation? If they questioned the validity of your evaluation, what kinds of things did they contest? On what kinds of things did they say, "Yes, this was absolutely right, and I will go to work on improving this area of my leadership"?

To understand evaluation we first had to take a look at accountability. *Accountability* usually referred to test scores that were reported (Reeves 2004). It has been taken a step further and is now tied into evaluations. If the school doesn't make the desired score on the state-mandated test, then teachers, administrators, and even superintendents will be held accountable.

Powell (2003) concludes that as accountability increases, the interest of accurate principal evaluations increases (also Albanese 2003). Albanese concludes from her study in Rhode Island that since the mandates are targeting accountability, a uniform method of evaluating principals should be developed.

In studying evaluation and student learning, Xu (2001) found that teachers and administrators listed accountability, teachers' growth, and improvement of curriculum and instruction as the most important parts of teacher evaluation. Wilson (1993) found that superintendents listed accountability as the most important reason for evaluating principals. He further found that 94 percent of the principals were evaluated by the superintendent.

According to Reeves (2004), true educational accountability makes you answer the following four questions:

- How are my students doing?

- Are the schools succeeding or failing?
- What works best to help students learn?
- Do test scores prove the effectiveness of educational programs?

Reeves states that "an accountability system that fails to address these common sense questions does not deserve the support and confidence of citizens or policy makers" (15). In essence, Reeves is saying that accountability systems must answer questions about student achievement, school performance, ways to help students learn, and determining educational effectiveness.

Communication is the essence of effective accountability. Communication should be continuous and proactive. Reeves (2004) argues that effective communications about accountability should answer the above four questions.

Effective accountability systems must be congruent, respect diversity, be accurate, be specific, have feedback, have universality, and be fair. Significant changes are planned in student assessment by district administration in collaboration with faculty. Catlin (2004) found that principal-evaluation systems do not provide feedback on their skills in order to improve performance.

Evaluation of administrative staff is an important part of the superintendent's job. Everyone is held accountable for student learning. Depending on the size of the district, the superintendent will evaluate all administrators (if it is a small district) or only assistant superintendents (if it's a large district). The evaluation process is delegated from the school board to the superintendent. The school board only evaluates the superintendent.

Evaluation serves an important service, as the school is continually monitoring itself so that students can learn to their maximum potential. Norton and colleagues (1996) state:

> Leadership in performance appraisal is instrumental in the implementation of school system goals and in meeting personal development needs within the system. In this sense, performance appraisal serves the formative objective of determining staff strengths and needs; strengths can be utilized optimally, and weaknesses can be remedied. (303)

Hoyle and colleagues (2005) concluded from a review of research that effective school leaders focus their efforts on four tasks:

- Building powerful forms of teaching and learning that are appropriate and effective with the children.
- Creating strong communities in schools characterized by a strong sense of affiliations, small learning-communities, and personalized environments in which students can succeed.

- Expanding students' social capital valued by schools by recognizing students' knowledge, values, preferences, behavioral habits, and attitudes toward schooling as assets rather than deficits.
- Nurturing the development of families' educational cultures to enhance student learning and success in school. (5–6)

Understanding where to focus their efforts allows superintendents to develop individualized evaluations plans with the administrators built on these four principles.

What does the superintendent evaluate when he/she is evaluating other supervisory staff? That depends upon their job descriptions and the adopted evaluation form (Conran 1989). The following are headings in an administrative evaluation instrument:

- Administration
- Planning
- Relationship with staff
- Relationship with community
- Professional growth and ethics
- Instructional leadership
- Personal characteristics
- Relationship with pupils

In addition, the instrument will have an area for professional growth. The superintendent uses this area to state the areas the administrator needs to grow or improve in.

Superintendents are evaluated by the job they do, and their performance is based on the administrators' performance. The *superintendent's evaluation cycle* (TASB 1998, 5) begins in May–July with "**Phase 1** (*Goal Setting*)":

- Board and superintendent having team building training.
- Reviewing the superintendent's job description and identifying performance indicators.
- Clarifying roles and articulating expectations for the board and superintendent.
- Reviewing the superintendent evaluation design and agreeing on a process, instrument, and timeline.
- Providing training for board on how to evaluate a superintendent.

Developing or revising the superintendent and board action plan August and September you begin **Phase 2** (*Campus/District Plan*):

- Reviewing performance data with the campus/district teams to assess needs and strengths.
- Adjusting campus/district plans as needed.
- Establishing processes to monitor campus/district plans.

Approving campus/district plans October and November begins **Phase 3** (*Formative Evaluation*):

- Monitoring and reporting on the progress of campus/district plans.
- Conducting formative evaluation exchanges between the superintendent and board.
- Adjusting the superintendent/board action plan and campus/district plans, as needed.

December and January begins **Phase 4** (*Formal Appraisal and Contract Renewal*):

- Conducting board and superintendent self-appraisals (optional).
- Review superintendent accountability report.

Conducting superintendent evaluation February–April is **Phase 5** (*Formative Evaluation*):

- Gathering qualitative data.
- Compiling quantitative and qualitative data into a formative and summative report.
- Conducting formative evaluation exchanges between the superintendent and the board.
- Start the phases over again.

Principal evaluation in North Carolina is completed by the principal as a self-assessment with the superintendent, in preparation for the summary evaluation meeting. The items evaluated are as follows:

Standard 1: Strategic Leadership
a. School vision, mission, and strategic goals
b. Leading change
c. School improvement plan
d. Distributive leadership
Standard 2: Instructional Leadership
a. Focus on learning and teaching, curriculum, instruction, and assessment
b. Focus on instructional time
Standard 3: Cultural Leadership
a. Focus on collaborative work environment

b. School culture and identity

c. Acknowledges failures, celebrate accomplishments, and rewards

d. Efficacy and empowerment

Standard 4: Human Resource Leadership

a. Professional development/learning communities

b. Recruiting, hiring, placing, and mentoring of staff

c. Teacher and staff evaluation

Standard 5: Managerial Leadership

a. School resources and budget

b. Conflict management and resolution

c. Systematic communication

d. School expectations for students and staff

Standard 6: External Development Leadership

a. Parent and community involvement and outreach

b. Federal, state, and district mandates

Standard 7: Micro-political Leadership

a. School executive micro-political leadership

Each of the areas are rated under the following categories: *developing*; *proficient*; *accomplished*; *distinguished*; *not demonstrated*. Under each of these standards, artifacts are suggested for proof of meeting the standard. This background provides a basis to discuss and answer the questions below from our study.

> Your first evaluation of supervisory staff: How accepting were your principals, etc., of your first evaluation? If they questioned the validity of your evaluation, what kinds of things did they contest? On what kinds of things did they say, "Yes, this was absolutely right, and I will go to work on improving this area of my leadership"?

We would hope that the evaluations of principals and other supervisory staff would follow in the direction described. Odds are, our respondents presented evaluation to their teachers or support staff in that vein. But sometimes administrators are like medical staff in hospitals: the most difficult patients.

Said one superintendent, in reply to our questionnaire:

> One principal was very accepting while another referred to it as "taking one up the _____." The disgruntled administrator later resigned for texting something to a student. The things that were agreed that need work dealt with the use of data when trying to improve student performance. I had a very supportive group of veteran administrators. They did not contest. The biggest problem was related to the way they evaluated their own staff.

Another superintendent said:

I gave both principals a copy of the evaluation tool three months prior to evaluating them. Part of the tool required them to evaluate themselves. There were no surprises. Since then, one of the principals was placed on an improvement plan. He did not agree with the issue, but agreed to proceed with the suggested plan. He was allowed to use resources he was familiar with to address deficiencies. Once he understood that his credibility among staff was questionable, he was more eager to address deficiencies.

I evaluate the central office administrative staff. [He seemed to be speaking of his present role as a large-school superintendent, instead of his first CEO job.] One of our Directors evaluates principals. The CO staff is pretty stout and there were no gaping holes in their professional acumen.

The first administrator I evaluated was "S," the principal of the high school. I knew that this would be a hard evaluation because I was told that the three "S's" ran the district. "S", the high school principal, "S," the athletic director, and "S," the board member, who later became board president.

The statement on the street was, "'S', the high school principal, knew what happened in the executive session of the board meeting the minute they came out of the meeting." This was true. "S," the board member, would call "S," the high school principal, and discuss the entire executive session with him.

Knowing this, I did my required evaluation of "S." Overall, "S" did a fine job but he did have a few items that was "in need of improvement." When I went over the evaluation with "S," the high school principal, he exploded. Needless to say that my experience in working with "S" was tenuous at best.

I tried my best to work with "S," the high school principal, but he was unteachable. I kept all of the documentation and within the first few months of my third year at that district, I made a statement to the board in executive session, "Either 'S' goes or I go." I had all of the documentation and I laid it out before the board. The board agreed, and when we came out of executive session, "S" was dismissed immediately.

"S", the board member, was not happy and after the vote to dismiss "S," the high school principal, made my life miserable. In answering the questions, "S" was not accepting of my evaluation. He was insubordinate which I feel was because of his relationship with the board member who was now the president.

Another described the first evaluations:

My first evaluation of the new assistant superintendent was an interesting experience. I had just hired the neighboring school district superintendent to be my assistant superintendent. He had previously worked in the district as a principal and was well respected. Overall, "K" received a very good evaluation but there were a few items I did mark Satisfactory.

The choices were Unsatisfactory, Satisfactory, and Outstanding. "K" came to my office and wanted to know why he didn't receive an Outstanding in all areas. He was pleasant and nice about it. He asked what he could do to improve. We had an excellent working relationship and because we demonstrated this positive working relationship, the district thrived.

Said another:

My first evaluation of a principal in one district in which I was a superintendent was difficult. I had nine principals and all of them were doing an excellent
job except for one. "T" could have been an excellent principal, but his treated
his teachers, support staff, and district employees with utter disregard and
contempt. "T" was president of the Middle School Principals Association in
the state, and because of his position, was named Middle School Principal of
the Year in the state.

I visited with "T" and told him he did an excellent job. He had to improve in
these "relationship" areas as I would not tolerate it and neither would the
district. He was put on an Improvement Plan. Morale in his building had sunk
to a new low. "T" became aggressive and was not teachable.

To make a long story short, he left the district a couple of years later; retired.
He was so angry with me he would not shake my hand when I went to his
building. I said we appreciated his work for children. He said, "I'll shake
hands with whom I want to shake hands." He took a principal position at
another district on the other side of the state and by September was fired.

Principals or central-office administrators who are positive with you about
their evaluations will be excellent employees. It's like with basketball
players. When the coach has the player work on a certain aspect of his or her
game and the player works hard to improve, you end up with a very good
basketball player who is a great team player. But in the same vein, if the
player doesn't listen and "gets an attitude," that player is usually not with the
team the next year or is relegated to the "end of the bench."

Heathfield (2011) writes:

Why is the evaluation process so painful for all participants? The superintendent is uncomfortable in the judgment seat. He knows he may have to justify
his opinions with specific examples when the administrator asks. He lacks skill
in providing feedback and often provokes a defensive response from the employee, who may justifiably feel he is under attack.

Consequently, superintendents avoid giving honest feedback which defeats the
purpose of the performance appraisal. In turn, the administrator whose performance is under review often becomes defensive. Whenever his performance is
rated as less than the best, or less than the level at which he personally per-
ceives his contribution, the superintendent is viewed as punitive.

Disagreement about contribution and performance ratings can create a conflict
ridden situation that festers for months. Most superintendents avoid conflict
that will undermine work place harmony. In today's team-oriented work environment, it is also difficult to ask people who work as colleagues, and sometimes even friends, to take on the role of judge and defendant. (1)

The administrator doing the evaluation knows that there will be a reaction to
the evaluation. The reactions can be of agreement, of defensiveness, of anger,
or of remorse. The administrator, in this case the superintendent, needs to

have the training on how to conduct effective performance evaluations, how to effectively communicate and listen, and how to deal with an angry administrator (Moore 2010).

There are also emotions felt by employees prior to the evaluation. *The Chronicle of Higher Education* (2008) had college professors write about their feelings regarding evaluation. One professor wrote, "Whenever an evaluation period is entered, I get anxious and paranoid . . . I run scenarios in my head that will give me a bad evaluation." The reply to this professor said, "A little anxiety is not bad—it shows that you care—but you can take steps to manage it."

Anxiety can be lessened by the superintendent going over the evaluation process and letting the administrators know what is expected of them. When the evaluation process is seen as a team process, then anxiety is minimal.

Sutton (2008) concluded from her review of the literature that most teachers expect to get high evaluations. Because of this expectation, administrators are reluctant to be honest because they do not want to go through the trials of an evaluation. This creates a culture of passivity and protection.

Teachers are reluctant to be honest about their difficulties as these could be seen as deficiencies. Additionally, teachers often don't trust the evaluator. Teachers experience stress because the uncertainty of the evaluations. Fear also comes from present politics and accountability. Teachers are fearful they will be held accountable for what they can't control (e.g., student behaviors, adequacy of teaching materials). They fear losing autonomy over their work and losing their jobs.

CHECKLIST FOR EVALUATING FACULTY AND STAFF

__ Plan evaluations for times that are not going to conflict with other major events on the calendar.

__ Schedule the time of day for meeting with the person being evaluated so that he or she will have time to process and reflect on the information after leaving your office.

__ Make sure that all who will be evaluated know at the beginning of the year your expectations.

__ Let the person being evaluated know your goals, purpose, and objectives for evaluation at the beginning of the meeting.

__ Don't send a teacher right back into a classroom if you want him or her to be able to process your suggestions.

__ Begin and end each meeting with something positive about the individual. For some, this may be challenging, but it will help the individual being evaluated positively accept the evaluation.

__ Check your ratings for possibility of skewed evaluation.

__ Have you been biased in any way?

__ Are your judgments of this employee based on the guidelines set forth in policy manuals, or your interpretations?

__ Always follow a faculty/staff policy manual that was approved by the school board.

__ Be *truly* open to the person being evaluated having a different view.

__ Be open to explanations they may have and information you may have been unaware of.

SUMMARY

Accountability drives the superintendent's evaluation. Superintendents use accountability as the most important reason for evaluating principals. According to Reeves (2004), true educational accountability answers the following questions: "How are my students doing?"; "Are the schools succeeding or failing?"; "What works best to help students learn?"; and "Do test scores prove the effectiveness of educational programs?"

Communication is the essence of effective accountability. Communication should be continuous and proactive. Principals or central-office administrators who are positive with you about their evaluations will be excellent employees, as this reflects their attitude and spirit of being teachable.

The administrator doing the evaluation knows that there will be a reaction to the evaluation. The reactions can be of agreement, defensiveness, anger, or remorse. Teachers are reluctant to be honest about their difficulties as these could be seen as deficiencies. Additionally, teachers often don't trust the evaluator.

REFLECTION QUESTIONS

1. Have I scheduled evaluations at a time that is particularly stressful and busy for me or those I am evaluating?
2. If so, is there a possibility to change the dates for evaluations? If no possibility of change, can I present them in a manner to make them less stressful?
3. Have I given the evaluation a few days after writing it, and then reread it to ensure that I still feel the same way in all areas?
4. Have I truly given as unbiased a report as possible?
5. Do I have specific documentation and/or examples of all areas on the evaluation (especially those areas that may need improvement)?

6. Am I going into the evaluation with the right attitude and purpose behind them, or do I have another agenda?
7. Are there any state guidelines or mandates for evaluations?

Chapter Twelve

Trends in Academic Achievement during the First Year(s)

> What kind of trend in academic achievement did you see your first year? To what extent did those trends reflect your leadership, as compared to a carry-over from the previous superintendent? After the first year, did you change some programs, approaches, methods, curricula, etc.? Describe what you did and the acceptance by staff, effects, etc.

It's no secret that we live in a world of instant gratification. The board hires a new superintendent and the expectation is that everything, including student test scores, will get better overnight. If only the public could see how indirect the influence of the superintendent can be as it reaches through several layers of administration to finally touch the students.

Board members want to see all of the students achieve. How can you make certain that students achieve? One of the first things you have to do is change the school culture. According to Renchler (1992), effectively managed businesses and effectively managed schools operate in much the same way. To effectively change a business or school you have to change the culture. Deal and Peterson (1990) define school culture as the deep patterns of values, beliefs, and traditions that have formed over the course of history.

> The elements of culture include vision, mission, beliefs and values.

- *Vision* is future-focused and directs the system toward what it desires to become.
- *Mission* defines the purpose of the system and why it exists.
- *Beliefs* are convictions and actions that staff want to live by. They are operating principles.

- *Values* are the personal attributes that are essential to model and promote by all employees of the system.

> The head, which gives direction, is the vision and mission. The heart, which gives energy is the beliefs and values. (Redalen 2010)

In summary, Redalen concludes:

> The evidence is clear—leaders can shape productive school cultures that set the context for student learning and increase staff efficacy . . . Judging school effectiveness is based on measures of student learning, it is the culture that mostly influences it.
>
> Goals and outcomes are essential but leaders must also inspire a culture that will enable goals to be reached. To attain the goals, various internal structures and processes need to be in place.
>
> These include:

- A focus on organizational health;
- Developing norms of collegiality;
- Fostering high staff morale;
- Communication;
- Decision-making processes; and
- Collaborative administrator and teacher leadership.

> A district's ability to continuously improve can be directly attributed to addressing and promoting these key elements. (21)

The state of Texas, like other states, is struggling to keep its adequate yearly progress rate up. Superintendents and school boards will be working extremely hard to keep the scores up in a time when finances have been cut. The Texas Education Association (2011) reported:

> Almost 5,600 Texas schools met the Adequate Yearly Progress (AYP) standards for the federal school rating system this year. This represents 66 percent of all Texas campuses.
>
> Schools and districts must have 80 percent or more of their students in grades 3–8 and 10 pass the Texas Assessment of Knowledge and Skills (TAKS) reading or English language arts test and 75 percent must pass the TAKS mathematics test to meet AYP. They also must achieve a 90 percent attendance rate or a 75 percent graduation rate, depending on the grade levels they serve. This year, 5,597 schools met AYP standards.
>
> AYP standards for 2011 are similar to the standards required to achieve a Recognized rating in the state accountability system. The state ratings were issued July 29.

Under the federal No Child Left Behind law, the standards must reach 100 percent passing on both reading and mathematics assessments by 2014 which requires a substantial increase in ratings standards each year in order to meet this requirement.

In 2010, 73 percent of the Texas students were required to pass the reading/ ELA test, while a 67 percent passing rate was needed on the mathematics test in order to met AYP. Seventy-eight percent of the schools met the standards under those criteria and benefited from the use of the Texas Projection Measure, which is not available to them this year.

"Statewide, our passing rates on the TAKS test largely held steady this year. Those results coupled with the elimination of Texas Projection Measure and rising federal standards caused fewer Texas schools to met AYP this year," said Commissioner of Education Robert Scott.

As a result, 50 percent of the Texas school districts meet AYP in 2011, compared to 78 percent the previous year.

The National Assessment of Educational Progress (NAEP) has been documenting trends since 1971. The NAEP provides results on subject matter achievement, instructional experiences, and school environment for populations of students and groups within those populations. NAEP does not provide scores for individual students or schools.

The National Center for Education Statistics, a department in the U.S. Department of Education, analyzes the NAEP assessments to see what the trends are. For example, results for nine-year-olds show that the average reading score was higher in 2004 than in any previous assessment period, and for seventeen-year-olds there was no statistical change in reading from 1999–2004. The difference between scores for white and black students has decreased when comparing 1971 to 2004.

The White House receives briefings on achievement indicators in international math and science, reading achievement, math achievement, dropout rates, public-school revenue and expenditures, and school crime and safety, as well as a host of others. The Center on Education Policy (2009) found from their analysis of student achievement that

- All subgroups showed more gains that declines in grade four at all three achievement levels—basic-and-above, proficient-and-above, and advanced.
- As measured by percentages of student scoring proficient, gaps between subgroups have narrowed in most states at the elementary, middle, and high school levels, although in a notable minority of cases gaps have widened.
- Most often gaps narrowed because the achievement of lower-performing subgroups went up rather than because the achievement of higher-performing subgroups went down.

- Gaps in percentages proficient narrowed more often for the Latino and African-American subgroups than for other subgroups.
- Although average scores indicate that gaps have narrowed more often than they have widened, average scores give a less rosy picture of progress in closing achievement gaps than percentages proficient. (3–4)

Renchler (1992) links student motivation to principal motivation. The principal is the curriculum leader of the school and sets the school climate. "If school leaders are equipped with the wisdom that comes from humility, sensitivity, and a constant reflection on the way that motivation functions in their own lives, it will probably be much easier for them to find ways to motivate their students" (2).

An environment that is conducive to learning will motivate the students. Changing a culture to motivate and achieve takes time and persistence, and, as the old adage goes, *change is a process, not an event.* The moral purpose (the intention of making a positive difference in the social environment) means closing the achievement gap (Fullan 2003). Renchler (1992) concludes that there are different approaches to improving motivation in educational settings. These are:

- Cultivating a school culture that establishes and celebrates the value of academic achievement;
- Restructuring our pedagogy so that new methods of instruction that might be effective can be tested;
- Understanding the various factors that shape an individual's propensity to be motivated or unmotivated. (19)

Renchler goes on to offer the steps listed in example 12.1 as ways to improve motivation in the school.

Example 12.1 Steps to Consider in Improve Student Motivation

- Analyze the ways that motivation operates in your own life and develop a clear way of communicating your understanding of it to teachers and students.
- Demonstrate to students how motivation plays an important role in your own life, both professionally and personally.
- Work with students, teachers, parents, and others to establish challenging but achievable school goals that promote academic achievement and the motivation that goes with it.
- Seek ways to demonstrate how motivation plays an important role in non-educational settings.

- Encourage instructional programs that offer alternatives to traditional educational practices with the idea that they might be more effective in motivating students.
- Make motivation a frequent topic of discussion among students, teachers, and other staff.
- Show students that success is important. Recognize the variety of ways that students can succeed. Reward success in all its forms.
- Develop or schedule teacher in-service programs that focus on motivation.
- Participate in administrator in-service programs that focus on motivation.
- Demonstrate through your own actions that learning is a lifelong process that can be pleasurable.
- Understand and promote the value of intrinsic motivation.
- Use extrinsic rewards systems wisely.
- Invite motivational speakers to your district.
- Ensure that restructuring programs address the issues related to student motivation.
- Get parents involved in discussing the issue of motivation.

Renchler (1992, 19)

An environment that encourages the principal to be the curriculum leader in the school will have a positive effect on student learning. The principal needs to be out of the office and making "classroom walk-throughs" to make certain that teachers are truly engaging students and motivating them to learn. If the students lack motivation, learning will be minimal. There are several ways a teacher can motivate students, beginning with strong classroom management. The following list describes some of these techniques:

- Have reasonable *expectations* for every class. Expect the students to learn, and they will.
- Show the students they can experience *success* in the classroom. Teachers can individualize instruction to meet each student's needs and learning ability.
- Show the students that what they are learning is relevant to their lives. *Relevance* gives meaning and purpose to the student's hard work.
- Ask *engaging questions*. These type of questions encourage the students to expand upon their existing knowledge.
- Use a variety of teaching strategies to *incorporate different learning styles*. Examples of different strategies are classroom discussion, cooperative group learning, direct instruction, individualized instruction, "think-pair-share," "popcorn" answers, inquiry-based teaching, using "ice-breakers," lecture, videotapes, panel of experts, role-playing, and so forth.

- *Rewards and privileges* are great motivators. Teachers can use a variety of methods to encourage students to participate and work hard.

Hutnik and Dehaney (2007) reported from their research that to get your school to come out on top, you have to focus on teacher quality. **High performing schools do the following things well**:

- They get the right people to become teachers.
- They develop these people into effective instructors.
- They put systems and targeted support in place to ensure that every child is able to benefit from excellent instructions. (16)

"The quality of an education system cannot exceed the quality of its teachers," write Hutnik and Dehaney (19). They go on to conclude that the "only way to improve outcomes is to improve instruction" (29). They then go on to say that top-performing schools are relentless in improving instruction. At the level of the teacher, three things have to happen:

- Individual teachers need to become aware of specific weaknesses in their own practice.
- Individual teachers need to gain understanding of specific best practices.
- Individual teachers need to be motivated to make the necessary improvements. This comes when teachers have high expectations, a shared sense of purpose, and a collective belief in their common ability to make a difference. . . .

To help improve instruction, **high-performing schools do the following**:

- Build practical skills during the initial training.
- Place coaches in schools to support teachers.
- Select and develop effective instructional leaders.
- Enable teachers to learn from each other. (30)

Strong leadership is important in producing improvement. Top-performing schools know what effective school leadership looks like and develop their principals into become instructional leaders. Developing effective instructional leaders in schools means doing the following, according to Hutnik and Dehaney (2007):

- Getting the right teachers to become principals.
- Developing instructional leadership skills.
- Focusing each principal's time on instructional leadership. (33)

They also state:

> **High-performing schools promote delivering for every child.** All of these systems have curriculum standards which set clear and high expectations for what students should achieve. To monitor this, these schools use two mechanisms:

- *Exams.* These tests what students know, understand and can do, providing an objective measure of actual outcomes at a high level.
- *School review.* These inspections assess the performance of a school against a benchmark set of indicators. They measure both outcomes and the processes which drive them. School reviews can be annual external reviews, self-evaluation with external review every three or four years, or self-review with occasional external review. This all depends on the individual school's performance. (32)

Said our own Dr. Roberts,

> In each of my superintendencies, I did see academic student achievement during my first year. The method I used was to continually in-service the principals, be visible in their buildings, and continually work to develop a culture in which student achievement was preeminent. I remember in my first superintendency that I communicated to my building principals at the first administrative meeting that I wanted to see growth in student achievement.
>
> I wanted to make certain that standardized-test scores were raised, student absenteeism was reduced, and teacher absenteeism declined. If the principals worked on developing an environment conducive to learning, in which the correct items were taught at the proper time, then test scores would increase.
>
> As one superintendent from a large metropolitan district told me, "How do we demonstrate learning if the teachers have taught the wrong things?" He went on to say that "the teacher could be an excellent teacher but if they taught the wrong thing, their standardized test scores would not reflect this."
>
> Second, I worked on making certain the teachers stayed in their buildings because from my research I found that teacher absenteeism was related to student achievement. In one district in which I was a superintendent, we had a policy that said the teacher could not take sick leave before a holiday. If the teacher had the flu or some other dreadful sickness, that was understandable, but what we were trying to curb was the teachers scheduling dentist visits and yearly physicals before holidays. This would extend their time away from the students, and the students suffered.
>
> Finally, I encouraged the principals and the teachers to vigorously contact parents so their children's absences were fewer. The principals were also encouraged to develop a quality school-home relationship. In essence, I asked that they develop a partnership with the parents. Again, through my research I found that students' absenteeism was related to student achievement. If the students felt we were truly interested in their well-being, then they would want to come to school and learn.

Overall, the principals and their staff were very supportive of my vision and mission for student success. If the previous superintendent's leadership style was not conducive to building an environment which would allow the teachers to be successful, that did not "spill over" to my administration. I did have to demonstrate through proven research that what I was proposing was sound and research based. I did not want to "fly by the seat of my pants," as that would have damaged my credibility.

I remember at my last superintendency, I took a group of stakeholders to look at a program called First Things First. Though the board didn't vote to adopt this program, I had a principal in the lowest-performing school in the district ask if she could incorporate the tenets of this program. I told her yes, and within a year, her school was performing at the top in the district.

In another district, I had another principal in a school that was underperforming come to me and say that she and the teachers wanted to incorporate an enhancement program into the school curriculum. She was the principal at a school that was almost 100 percent Hispanic. The program was research based, and I asked her to present the program to the board of education so we could get approval as a pilot program. The student scores improved dramatically after the first year.

The major things that I did to get acceptance from the staff were the following:

- I demonstrated a servant-leadership style.
- I showed concern for their well-being.
- I communicated to them frequently.
- I frequently visited their buildings so they would get to know me.
- I treated them with respect.
- I kept myself well read in the latest research and methods so I could demonstrate competency.
- I provided opportunities for them to grow professionally.
- I kept a positive spirit with them when they were experiencing a "down" day.
- I recruited quality staff that would "fit in."

Said one Texas superintendent:

> We were able to improve in several areas of TAKS [Texas Assessment of Knowledge and Skills] testing. We added staff in critical areas to reduce teacher/student ratio. We added a sign-on bonus and stipend for secondary math and science which enabled us to keep and hire quality teachers. More time and resources were committed to university Interscholastic League academic competitions, which also helped to improve student achievement. Because of turnover among faculty, we did several things to improve the climate and "family feel" for teachers in the district.

Another superintendent did not say much about the specifics of the achievement-test scores, but talked more about the direction of the district during his first year: "Probably the only thing we have changed is trying to emphasize technology as a learning tool. We don't want the teachers to get caught up with the test scores; we want them to prepare students for the real future."
   Said another:

> High school improved to "Recognized." Elementary improved to "Exemplary." It was not so much "me" as it was a team effort from all administrators and teachers. We did not change the curriculum because what they were doing was working. I simply had the administrators monitor teacher performance more closely.

A superintendent in Western Arkansas declared:

> I am very much a "servant leader," I live on campus. The staff regularly sees me working and I am on each campus daily. They are eager to voluntarily do their part any time they are asked to do something. Our school makes adequate yearly progress (AYP). The high school is on alert status this year for literacy. I pointed out to the staff that all literacy teachers would go through literacy lab, comprehensive literacy approach training. They all eagerly agreed. Also, we are doing target assessments on a quarterly basis and thoroughly analyze data. This provides meaningful feedback to teachers and allows deficiencies to be addressed by the teacher and by using the JEDI remediation/intervention software. They also receive trend data from them after benchmark data are gathered annually.

Said another, "The trends that I saw academically had to do with increased proficiency in standardized test scores. This was due to nothing that I might have done. It was due to refocusing and realignment by a talented group of curriculum specialists."

CHECKLIST FOR DETERMINING THE TRENDS IN ACADEMIC ACHIEVEMENT

   __ Gather research on test scores for the schools, district, state, and national level soon after arriving, to determine where you stand.
   __ Determine if you meet state goals and requirements.
   __ Determine if the school board has preset goals for the district.
   __ If no goals are preset, begin the process of goal setting.
   __ Evaluate the district's mission, along with the board and your visions, to see if they all align.
   __ Determine if mission, vision, and academic-achievement goals align.

__ Know the research on what *really* improves academic achievement.
__ Create a plan that aligns all of these factors.
__ Set a time frame for achievement of said goals.
__ Reevaluate the plan annually.

SUMMARY

We live in a world of instant gratification. The board hires a new superintendent and the expectation is that everything, including student test scores, will get better overnight. The community and board members want to see all of the students achieve.

How can you make certain that students achieve? One of the first things you have to do is change the school culture. The elements of culture include vision, mission, beliefs, and values. An environment that is conducive to learning will motivate the students. Changing a culture to motivate and achieve takes time and persistence, and, as the old adage goes, *change is a process, not an event.*

Hutnik and Dehaney (2007) reported from their research that to get your school to come out on top, you have to focus on teacher quality. "High performing schools do the following things well: They get the right people to become teachers. . . . They develop these people into effective instructors. . . . They put systems and targeted support in place to ensure that every child succeeds" (16).

Effective first-year superintendents were authentic, got the people in the right places, realigned key personnel, upgraded technology, found additional resources to hire competent people in critical areas, focused the staff development, built community, and developed the professional learning-community concept.

REFLECTION QUESTIONS

1. Do I know what level (academically) the district is at yet? Is the district *academically unacceptable, academically acceptable, recognized*, or *exemplary*? From a study of district data, what improvements need to be made? How does each school rate within the district?
2. Have we been making adequate yearly progress?
3. What are the board's expectations of me?
4. Are these expectations realistic? Why or why not?
5. Is data-driven decision making utilized in the district? Why or why not? What are the benefits of data-driven decision making?

6. Discuss the benefits of professional learning communities.
7. What trends in education have I seen in the past and present? What would I recommend future superintendents should know and be aware of?

Chapter Thirteen

Knowing When It Is Time to Move

HOW DO WE KNOW IT'S TIME TO MOVE OR RETIRE?

Many superintendents wonder if they should keep working in their current district or if they should leave. It's not uncommon for superintendents to change districts. Czaja and Harman (1997) found in Texas that the superintendency turnover rate was almost 19 percent in 1992, but had leveled out at 15.4 percent in 2009, according to the Texas Association of School Boards. Byrd and colleagues (2006) reported in their review of the literature that in regard to superintendent tenure, it was found that in North Carolina, the average tenure for a superintendent was six to seven years (Natkin et al. 2002). The average national tenure for urban superintendents was 2.75 years (Council of Great City Schools). The average tenure for superintendents among all sizes of school districts was four to five years, according to a study by the Council of Urban Boards of Education. In another study of all sizes of district, the average tenure was five to six years (Glass 2000).

Reasons superintendents leave a district can be narrowed down to three: retirement, performance, and personal. The personal reason is the one that is intriguing. A search of doctoral dissertations reveals that there have been over 400 dissertations written since the 1950s about superintendent-board relations. Czaja and Harman (1997) reported, after interviewing superintendents who had left, that the main reasons for leaving were related to either relationships with the school board, enticing opportunities, or personal factors.

Byrd and colleagues (2006) reported from their study that one of the most daunting tasks facing a superintendent is **student achievement**. This is a board's primary mission. When a new board member was elected to the board, the first question she asked me was, "How are we going to make certain that students succeed?" and the second question was, "Are we making AYP [adequate yearly progress]?" She was concerned, as we were a Title I district with a large minority population. She had attended the school before it began to change and remembered it before it turned into a Title 1 district. She had a hard time of understanding the differences in needs because of demographic changes and saw everyone as herself.

The second "fly in the ointment" is **superintendent-board relationships**. When problems arise, which they will, this strains at the superintendent-board relationship; and if there are enough problems, the bond will break. School-board micromanaging will break this bond. Some boards want a superintendent they can control, and if they feel that they cannot control the superintendent, then the bond will break. Many superintendents report that board members meddling into business that does not come under the scope of the superintendency will break the bond. Board members sometimes "meddle" because they see factors in the superintendent's performance that warrant the intrusion. A quality relationship between the board and superintendent has been found to be a key cornerstone for high student achievement (Goodman & Zimmerman 2000). Dalton (1984) reported from his study that superintendents in North Carolina identified *self-interest, withholding information, power, personality characteristics,* and *lack of well-defined role expectations* as factors that will erode board-superintendent relations. He went on to say that only one-fourth of superintendents who leave their position will go on and get another position. Finally, from his study, he found that the size of the school district, type of school district, age of the superintendent, and educational level of superintendent did not influence turnover rate.

A third reason that superintendents leave is they **feel pressure on multiple fronts due to performance**. Today the superintendent has to lead and guide challenging, dynamic systems while responding to social and political pressures. Rohland (2002) speculates that the high standards coupled with the people-intensive nature of districts explains why the job is so demanding. In addition, each step up the ladder you go, the more criticism you will receive. *You will not be able to satisfy everyone.* Teachers, parents, students, other administrators, board members, community members, and so forth make the possibility for conflict likely. Havery (2003) concludes that superintendent success lies in learning from the attacks and criticism without being defeated in the process.

There are other reasons that will help push a superintendent out of the door, which are:

a. **Time** is one of those factors affecting the superintendency. It is a valuable resource and can quickly be used up by special-interest groups' demands and community pressures. In a study of superintendents, CASE (2003) found that the average superintendent put in over eighty hours of work a week. *The superintendency is a labor-intensive job.*

b. In regard to superintendent self-perception of effectiveness, **lack of finance knowledge and finances** was cited as a major reason for inhibiting effectiveness and pushing a superintendent out of the door (CASE 2000).

c. **Demands and mandates** without the resources to make them come to pass are key reasons superintendents cannot be effective and reasons they will leave.

d. Finally, **short tenure** has hindered a superintendent's effectiveness. The district faculty and staff know that all they have to do is "tread water," as you'll be leaving pretty soon.

According to Dr. Roberts, "I had one assistant superintendent say to me, 'I've worked here twenty years and you're my tenth superintendent.' I had a real uphill battle to fight. The superintendent became the scapegoat for the community's problems. I told the board during the interview that if they felt I wasn't what they wanted, I would pleasantly leave. If they wanted me to leave because they did something illegal, immoral, or unethical, then I would 'fall on the sword for that'—stay and fight for the students."

When Allen (1996) studied this leaving phenomenon, she found that the positive reasons women left the superintendency were *marriage, new job opportunities* in larger communities, *freedom from schedules,* or *better pay.* Among the negative reasons that female superintendents left were *politics, superintendent-board relations, finances, opposition to instructional programs, ethical/moral/legal problems, working conditions,* and *gender-related problems.* Tallerico and colleagues (1993), when studying women superintendents, found out that the four main reasons they left involuntarily were *school board problems, union problems, role overload* (i.e., too much demand on their time), and *ethical/moral differences.* Working relationship with the board president, ability to get decisions made at the board level, and superintendent-board relations were statistically significant factors in determining superintendent tenure. In order of significance, the following factors in the area of board relations will diminish the superintendent's length of tenure: not being able to work with the board president, not being able to get decisions from the board, and poor superintendent-board communication.

Superintendents know that their position is heavily fraught with politics and their "fit" in the community. This occupation has very little security; and superintendents have fewer benefits than corporate CEOs, face greater criticism, and face greater complexities (Cooper et al. 2000; Goodman & Zimmerman 2000). Russo (1980) looked at factors that were identified as contributing to the retention or dismissal of the urban superintendent. What he found was that boards and superintendents gave different reasons for the dismissal. There was more agreement between the board and retained superintendents. He concluded that feelings of cooperation and trust, good personal relations, and a general agreement as to what things were really important appeared to be the overriding factors for superintendents that were retained. Maybe the difference in answers from the dismissed superintendents and their boards explains why these superintendents were not retained.

Superintendent-board relations has been written about in numerous studies (Alsbury 2003; Bracket 1995; Castallo 2003; Kitchens 1994; MASB 2005; McAdams 1996; Patrick 2006; these are only a very few of the authors who have written about superintendent-board relations). The following list consists of examples from newspaper articles about superintendents who are leaving or will be leaving their districts. The reasons are many.

- "Mt. Vernon Superintendent says failed school referendum had nothing to do with his retirement."
- "DeKalb says dumping superintendent will be cheaper this time."
- "Superintendent says the time is right to leave school district."
- "Superintendent runs Senath-Poorman school system into the ground and almost to bankruptcy."
- "Urban superintendents prove hard to hold on to."
- "Owen J. Roberts superintendent fired and community is shocked."
- "East Detroit Board of Education fired superintendent for failing to supervise the finances that were spinning out of control."
- "Kiamichi Tech superintendent was shocked when he was fired as the school was just award the Gold Star award."
- "Del Mar superintendent fired despite protest which was due to a material breach of her contract."

Insight into the frequency of superintendent turnover was best reported by Shirley Jinkins in the *Fort Worth Star-Telegram* in 2010 when she wrote:

> Superintendent Kay Waggoner is leaving the Grapevine-Colleyville school district for one twice its size, the Richardson school district. She has been in Grapevine-Colleyville for five and a half years, and according to district officials, community members and Waggoner herself, it has been a good fit. As basically the chief executive of a small corporation—the school district has a budget of $141.9 million with 1,650 employees and 13,621 students—it may not seem like a long time to be in charge. But Waggoner, who said she was not seeking a new job, is leaving corporate-style—she was recruited by Richardson for the open job. Research shows that Waggoner's tenure in Grapevine is typical for a 21st-century superintendent.

Observers say that frequent turnover is inevitable. An urban superintendent must manage staff, work effectively with the school board and boost educational standards and accountability. "The superintendency is a difficult, difficult job, and some people just get worn out," said Bob Griggs of North Richland Hills. He now is a superintendent search consultant after retiring in 1993 as superintendent of the Birdville district. "The stress is enormous on a day-to-day basis." Often superintendents are hired in hopes that they will be a district's "savior." But while national averages show it takes about five years for a successful new superintendent to turn around a troubled district, urban superintendents are only around for an average of 3 1/2 years.

Mac Bernd, who retired two years ago as the Arlington superintendent after serving 10 years in that post, said school boards have become more politically active, making the top jobs dicier even under the best of circumstances. Superstar superintendents can quickly lose their luster. Hector Montenegro, Bernd's highly touted successor in Arlington, resigned under pressure in 2008 after only six months on the job when his alliances with educational foundations became an issue.

The Dallas school district has been through a revolving door of superintendents. Current Superintendent (at the time of this writing) Michael Hinojosa has not been offered the obligatory contract extension during his most recent review. Schools are pressed to offer more services of all kinds, education financing has become more difficult, and regulations more complex. "Just in my 10 years in Arlington, the change in the accountability system was profound," Bernd said. "You had to answer to the demands of both the feds and the state, and sometimes those were conflicting."

Superintendents in the Tarrant County (Texas) area are paid well, but in terms of the CEO of a midsize company, it isn't excessive. School districts are often their city's top employer with bigger operating budgets than those of the municipal government. Fort Worth Superintendent Melody Johnson's base salary is $328,950, and Arlington's Jerry McCullough's base salary is $235,000. Northwest chief Karen Rue makes $215,812, and Southlake Carroll's David Faltys gets $200,000. Former Crowley Superintendent Greg Gibson's salary was $179,449. His new assignment at Schertz-Cibolo-Universal City pays $183,000, and Jeri Pfeifer at Everman makes $161,500.

"Early on, you've got to make a decision on whether you're career-bound or place-bound," Bernd said. Career-bound superintendents make moves for bigger districts and higher salaries, while place-bound ones live where they're content, with less money and less opportunity for advancement. "I was career-bound when I went to Arkansas," said Bernd, who only stayed in that assignment for a year. It was his second district. "But when I went to Arlington I was place-bound."

Typically there are about 150 superintendent vacancies a year among Texas' 1,030 school districts, said Mayo Neyland, a consultant with the Texas Association of School Boards executive search firm. He is currently coordinating superintendent searches for both the 15,000-student Crowley and 33,000-student Irving districts. Smaller districts are usually where superintendents are developing, Neyland said, and moving up and away.

"Superintendent turnover in the Tarrant region in 2010–2011 actually isn't as high as in other areas of Texas," said Richard Ownby, director of Education Service Center Region XI, which is based in Fort Worth. The 10 counties in the region have about half the turnover rate of the state average, he said, and of the 77 school districts within the area, only 10 had a superintendent switch last year.

"Twenty-five percent of the new superintendents in Tarrant County have been hired from within," Ownby said, mirroring a trend of some cash-strapped districts forgoing the search-firm route altogether to save anywhere from $6,500 to $30,000 in fees. Before 1995, Texas superintendents once had a state-mandated pay scale that discouraged moves to other districts since the small raise was not worth the cost of relocation. Now, the era of hometown superintendents staying at districts for decades, such as Crowley's Sidney Poynter, who served the district for 40 years, are definitely gone.

Rather than career-length longevity, Bernd said, school boards should look at whether the candidate is likely to stay long enough to accomplish what the board wants. "Boards can become complacent about salary," Bernd said. "They will let a good superintendent get away, then pay more money for a new superintendent to come in."

Roberts (2010) recommended that even though you've been hired in a new position, don't let your résumé grow stale. Keep it updated and remember that this is the first day of your starting to look for another superintendency. That advice was given to him by a wise veteran superintendent, and even though he never sent out his résumé the first year or the second year, he always kept it up-to-date and frequently looked at Web sites that listed openings, as he knew the superintendency was a position in which you never knew when you would "accidentally step on a land mine."

When you've come to the conclusion that it's time to move on, then it's time to polish the résumé and brush up on your interviewing skills. The résumé should sell you into your next superintendency. Enelow and Boldt (2006) recommend that you understand six simple truths:

- *Write to the Future.* Write toward your next superintendency. Don't rehash your past experiences. This is probably the single most important strategy for resume writing.
- *Know Who You Are.* It's not possible to write an effective resume without knowing what your object is. To fulfill *Truth #1*, you must have a job goal in mind. Making comparison lists such as your likes/dislikes, what you do well/don't do well, and so forth will help you see who you are.
- *Strategy and Positioning are Key.* Your resume has to present you as the best candidate for the superintendency for which you are apply so you will receive a job interview and/or offer. This is done by positioning yourself as how you want to be perceived. In essence, the

resume must portray the BEST YOU for the superintendent position you seek. For a superintendent's position, "You need a resume that looks sharp and upscale, clearly highlighting your achievements and contributions, and demonstrates the depth of your leadership experience" (15).

- *Sell It; Don't Tell It.* In essence, "resume writing is all about sales, marketing, and brand positioning" (16). You have to think of yourself as a special superintendent that is right for that district and is the solution for that district. Your goal is to "develop the best plan for marketing yourself to those districts who have a demand for the skills and qualifications you offer" (16).
- *Keywords Rock!* Keywords are "buzz words" found in your profession. They identify the essential skill, knowledge, and expertise that distinguish someone in the superintendency. Incorporate the keywords throughout your resume.
- *There Are No Rules for Resume Writing.* This provides you great flexibility but the following guidelines will help you. (1) Include a work experience section on your resume. (2) Include an education section on your resume. (3) Highlight skills and qualifications. (4) Start your resume with a career summary. (5) Write in the first person. (6) Beware of absolutes. How long should your resume be? Long enough to tell the prospective employer your story.

Enelow and Boldt (2006) recommend that you avoid the critical mistakes listed below:

- Never overstate the truth on your resume.
- Never include negative information on your resume.
- Never include salary information on your resume.
- Never present a resume with errors.
- Never include reason for leaving a job on your resume.
- Never submit a resume that is difficult to read.
- Never include a vague or unclear objective on your resume.
- Never send a resume with handwritten comments.
- Never send along supporting documentation with your resume.
- Never send a resume without a cover letter.

Isaacs (2010) lists common resume blunders. Make certain you avoid these:

- Too focused on job duties rather than responsibilities.
- Flowery or general objective statement.
- Too short or too long.
- Using personal pronouns and articles (DON'T).

- Listing irrelevant information.
- Using a functional format rather than a chronological formal.
- Not including references. [**NOTE:** We recommend that you leave the references off of the main resume but enclose a reference list as a separate page in your application package.]
- Typos.

When it comes to listing your accomplishments, whether on your résumé or a separate list as part of the résumé package, Thompson (2010) has the following to say:

If you were an employer looking at a new college graduate's resume, which of the following entries would impress you more?

- Wrote news releases, or
- Wrote 25 news releases in a three-week period under daily deadlines.

Clearly, the second statement that quantifies effort and results is more appealing. These following rules will enhance your chances for acquiring an interview:

- List "Accomplishments" not "Responsibilities." Every administrator has similar responsibilities. It is what you did with those responsibilities that sets your resume apart from other applicants.
- Before listing your accomplishments make a list of ways you have saved money, secured additional funding, managed money effectively, improved district performance, reduced dropouts, etc.
- Now develop a statement in measurable terms showing how you were successful. The statement should begin with an action verb, i.e. developed, initiated, organized, etc. and should include, if possible, quantifiable results. Never use a personal pronoun (i.e. I, my, etc.).

Below is an example of how an "Accomplishments" section might look when listed under one of the job you have held:
ACCOMPLISHMENTS:

- Initiated a *Stay in School* campaign that cut the dropout rate in half and increased attendance by a percentage point. This action resulted in $87,000 annual increase in state aid.
- Increased the number of minority faculty members by 42 percent.

- Moved the district from *Acceptable* to *Recognized* status in three years with all sub populations increasing their scores on all tests by a minimum of 22 percentage points.

Superintendent positions differ according to different districts. Once you've identified a superintendent position that is of interest to you be prepared to expect an intensive process that involves meetings with multiple constituents (parents, administrators, community members, school board members, students, and so forth). Each of these groups will have a different set of questions, concerns, and expectations. For these reasons, it's essential that you do your homework before you show up for the interview. Your goal is to "sell yourself." To do that effectively, do the following:

- Be well prepared. Do your research: Know about the community, the district, and the history before you arrive. Try to find the district philosophy to understand the heart and soul of the district. Have a friend or colleague critique your answers. Anticipate general questions and prepare for hard questions.
- Don't ever forget during the interview process that your primary job is student success.
- Interviewing is a two-way process. Be ready to ask some questions.
- Don't try to bluff yourself through an interview. Don't be a phony.
- Ask your colleagues for inside information about the district. Use your network of superintendents.
- Be able to articulate your skills to the district's needs and desires. Be prepared to answer succinctly. As one superintendent told me, "Don't bloviate."
- Come across as self-confident in yourself and in your body language. Be self-confident but not arrogant. Keep good eye contact. Be cordial and friendly.
- Take key materials along to the interview.
- Don't come across as being overly nervous or unsure.
- Be on time to the interview. The recommendation is that you arrive approximately 10 minutes before the interview.
- Dress professionally and have great hygiene. Especially make certain your breath smells fresh. Don't forget that etiquette is important. Look the part of a superintendent.
- Convince the board that you are the best one for the position and that you have an interest living and working in the community.
- Have a short list of questions to ask the board. I would recommend that you have six prepared but be able to limit it to three due to time constraints.

- Portray relationships, relationships, relationships.

Table 13.1 lists sample superintendent interview questions. It is recommended that you keep a file of these questions, with answers, so you are prepared for every interview.

In summary, Thomas (2010), in his interview of search executive consultants, reported that they recommend that the candidates need to be well prepared. Benjamin Canada, a search consultant said, "What you say in an interview will make a difference" (1).

The second piece of advice these search consultants gave was that the candidate needs to understand the different processes and learn how to network. This will improve their chances of finding the right match. For search consultants, the search is not over until the board is happy with the candidate. "The ability to find the right candidate is predicated upon having an understanding of what a district is looking for, the development of a profile, and the screening of candidates that match the profile. It is important that candidates don't apply for the sake of applying, but that candidates only apply for positions they really want" (Thomas 2010, 1). The tips provided were practical tips for anyone going for their first job interviews: Know the certification requirements; pay attention to what you put on paper; and be honest. The person in the interview should be the same person on the job.

Thomas Leahy, a search consultant, said, "Sometimes candidates are too eager. I suggest they under-promise and over-deliver" (Thomas 2010, 1). Finally, the superintendent needs to have an awareness of what the search process looks like. Some processes are 100 percent confidential, but technology and the Internet have made information about candidates accessible for the general public, and this can impact the search process. Thomas (2010) goes on to report that search firms will ask, "What is it I need to know?" about the candidate. The reputation of the search firm depends on its ability to effectively vet candidates. Eliza Holcomb said, "Boards don't want to be blindsided" (1). The search executives conclude that the success of working with the school board is predicated upon relationships. Finally, Dawn Miller advised, "Get to know the search firms and make yourself available. Learn what search firms look for" (1). Glenn (2008) concluded from his study that search consultants perceive that communication skills and relationship skills are the most important characteristics of potential superintendents. According to Glenn (2008), search consultants are the gateway to the superintendency because they dictate who will make it to the interview.

No chapter on this topic would be complete without a discussion of *The Peter Principle* (Peter & Hull 1969). *The Peter Principle* says that in a hierarchically structured administration, people tend to be promoted up to their level of incompetence. This principle was built through observations. New employees usually start at the bottom and when they prove that they are

Table 13.1. Sample superintendent interview questions

Number	Question
1	Describe the process you use to build leadership skills throughout the district, thus assisting principals to lead in a standards-based environment.
2	Provide evidence of how the district monitors the teaching of standards in each school.
3	How does the district ensure that correctives and enrichments are provided to all students who fail to meet or exceed the standards?
4	How does the district use assessment results?
5	How do you monitor that school administrators use assessment results to make instructional decisions? *Provide evidence.*
6	Discuss the process you use to assure that school improvement plans are • progressing; • monitored; • adjusted; • result in positive trends in meeting student performance standards.
7	Across your district, describe how the professional development programs/ initiatives have impacted the knowledge, skills, and practices of educators. *Be specific.*
8	From a district perspective, explain how student-performance standards affect planning and prioritizing of facilities, fiscal, technological, and human-resource projects.
9	What is done at the district level to notify, recruit, and involve all parents and interested community members in advisory roles? Address the following: • program planning • goal/standards setting and alignment • implementing of standards • assessing priorities/needs, including budget priorities
10	How does the district train parents in support of student learning?
11	Explain the district's plan to integrate technology across the curriculum. What training is being provided by the district to facilitate this goal?
12	Explain the district's efforts to train teachers and administrators in procedures to assist at-risk students.
13	How do you ensure climate-assessment results are used in school-improvement planning across the district?

competent, they are promoted. This can go on forever until employees reach positions in which they are no longer competent. They try to remain until or unless they are removed.

Heylighen (2000) writes:

At that moment the process typically stops, since the established rule of bu-
reaucracies make that it is very difficult to "demote" someone to a lower rank,
even if that person would be much better fitted and more happy in that lower
position. The net result is that most of the higher levels of a bureaucracy will
be filled by incompetent people, who got there because they were quite good at
doing a different . . . task than the one they are expected to do. (1)

Lazear (2001) echoes this when he observes that many people perform worse
after receiving a promotion. He offers two explanations for this: The first is
that promotion incentives slack off after the promotion has been granted. The
second explanation is that after being promoted, an individual's output is
expected to fall. He argues that you regress to the mean, which means productivity will decline.

Lazear (2004) later clarified these observations when he said, "Being
promoted implies that future ability will be lower, on average. Firms opti-
mally account for the regress bias in make promotion decisions, but the effect
is never eliminated. The Peter Principle is a necessary consequence of any
promotion rule . . . this explains why movie sequels are worse than the
original" (S141).

Pluchino and colleagues (2009) concluded from their study that the Peter
Principle is unavoidable. They recommend that to avoid the Peter Principle,
you must promote a randomness. Kedrosky (2009), on reading the study by
Pluchino and colleagues, mused that the only way you could foil the Peter
Principle was by using "darts."

Sutton (2010) argues that we shouldn't give up and start promoting leaders randomly, because this challenges life's rationality. Canada (1989), in
studying superintendent-board relations, concluded that "a failure of superin-
tendent/board relationship is seldom due to technical incompetence; the
cause has to do more with matters of equitable treatment and openness, and
that in the long-run may be more important variables in top leadership than
variables related to technical competence" (1).

To avoid the Peter Principle without pain, Frank (2002) recommends that
you promote from within. To promote from within, Frank says the following
questions need to be asked:

- Which employees have had the highest ratings within the past six to
  eighteen months?
- Who has exhibited the initiative to perform above and beyond the
  required job duties?
- Is the employee willing to take on a leadership role with additional
  responsibilities?
- Has the employee's performance improved on a consistent basis or
  fluctuated?

- Does the employee exhibit leadership behaviors or have the capacity to perform well within key supervisor/management competencies?

In regard to the last questions, Frank (2002) states that the following common leadership competencies should be considered when evaluating employees:

- Problem solving and decision making
- Managing performance and delegating
- Communication
- Planning and organizing
- Respect and trust

These leadership competencies need to be observed in the people who will be promoted. Finally, Frank (2002) recommends that in addition to performance appraisals, aptitude or personality tests, interviews, assessment tools, and commitment need to be used. Frank concludes, "There will be skill gaps when promotion occurs. But thousands of supervisors and managers have been placed in their current positions without the proper training or tools to help them take on their new responsibilities . . . When the process is done right, employee productivity will improve, turnover will be reduced, and costs will decrease" (2).

Shimoji (1999) concludes that demotion is rarely observed in practice for incompetent workers. He offers two reasons that demotions are rare. The first reason is that there is a cost to demoting workers because this would send a productive worker to another firm, and replace that worker with an unproductive one. The second reason is to conceal the identity of the incompetent worker to an outside firm which may employ him/her in the future.

Riggio (2010) asks the question, "Why there are so many incompetent leaders?" He offers the following reasons:

- We don't do a good job of selecting leaders.
- We rely too much on seniority.
- Our bureaucratic structures drag us down.
- We settle for mediocrity.

To overcome the Peter Principle, Riggio (2010) recommends that you "utilize the best hiring practices, work hard to evaluate everyone's performance, and engage in meaningful leader development within the organization" (1).

CHECKLIST FOR WHEN IT'S TIME TO MOVE AND PREPARE YOURSELF FOR THE NEXT SUPERINTENDENCY

___ Student achievement is the district's mission and is declining or not improving.

___ Superintendent-board relationships are negative.

___ Demand on time is too great.

___ Past catches up with you.

___ Moral and ethical differences.

___ An incumbent board member has been defeated.

___ Teacher's union is dissatisfied with you.

___ Pressure is felt on multiple fronts.

___ People are becoming increasingly dissatisfied with you.

___ Résumé is up-to-date.

___ Executive presence has been coached.

___ Interview questions are answered and saved in a database.

___ Districts where you'll interview have been studied.

___ You are current in education trends, issues, and finances.

___ References are up-to-date.

___ Placement office credentials are up-to-date.

SUMMARY

In the superintendency, changing locations is a fact of life. Anyone who aspires to the office should be prepared to relocate every few years. "Adventures in moving" can happen for reasons not intended by a superintendent, or they can be matters of a CEO's choice. A certain size of district with certain characteristics should be your focus. Not everyone should aspire to be an urban superintendent overseeing the learning of 500,000 students. Really consider your personal life goals and needs when beginning to think about a change. Also, look at the goals and history of the district you are considering. Do they fit with your beliefs, core values, goal, and life mission? This information will help you to find a fit that will be more productive for both you and the district.

REFLECTION QUESTIONS

1. Why am I considering a change?
2. Do I *want* to move or do I *need* to move?

3. Would moving to a new district really be worth the change if it is just for more money?
4. How long has it been since I updated my résumé?
5. A résumé is one thing, a vita is another. Is mine a résumé (typically two pages or less) or a vita (twenty pages)? Am I prepared to give a prospective employer either one upon request?
6. Regarding the Peter Principle, do I know my limits? And on the other end of the spectrum, what is the minimum amount of challenge I will need to feel like I can make a difference in the life of a district?

References

Albanese, L. J. (2003). Identifying and assessing current practices in principal evaluation. Doctoral dissertation, Boston University.

Anastasia, C. (2007). Humor and leadership. Coolspark.blogspot.com Retrieved from http://icoolspark.blogspot.com/2007/06/humor-and-leadership.html

Angry parents confront school board with tales of bullying. (2010, October 13). At www.wmbfnews.com.

Archer, K., and A. Eger. (2011). Union bond issue passes, area runoffs set. At tulsaworld.com (accessed February 14, 2011).

Arneson, S. (2010, February 22). How to run an effective staff meeting. *Leadership Examiner*. At www.examiner.com.

Associated Press (2004, April 5). Muslim student, Oklahoma district settle hijab lawsuit. At www.fac.org.

Avolio, B., Howell, J., & Sosik, J. (1999). A funny thing happened on the way to the bottom line: Humor as a moderator of leadership style effects. *Academy of Management Journal*, 42(2), 219-27.

Baldoni, J. (2009). Humility as a leadership trait. HBR Blog Network. Retrieved from http://Blogs.hbr.org/baldoni/2009/09/humility_as_a_leadership_trait.html

Bar, M., Neta, M., & Linz, H. (2006). Very first impressions. *Emotion*. 6(2). 269-78.

Billing, K. (2010, May 13). An interview with former superintendent Sharon McClain. *Del Mar Times*. At www.delmartimes.net.

Black, J., and F. English. (1986). *What they don't tell you in schools of education about school administration*. Lancaster, PA: Technomic.

Burn, J. (Editor, 2004). *Encyclopedia of Leadership*. Thousand Oaks, CA: Sage.

Byrd, J., Drews, C., & Johnson, J. (2006). Factors impacting superintendent turnover: Lessons from the field. ERIC. ED 493287.

Cannon, L. (2010, October 6). Parents complain CFISD isn't doing enough to stop bullying. At www.khou.com.

Catlin, M. E. V. (2004). Assessing leadership competencies. Doctoral dissertation, University of Oregon.

Center on Education Policy (2009). *Are achievement gaps closing and is achievement rising for all?* Author. At www.cep-dc.org.

Chapman, C. H. (1997). *Becoming a superintendent: Challenges of school district leadership*. Upper Saddle River, NJ: Prentice-Hall.

Chronicle of Higher Education (2008). Evaluation anxiety blog. At chronicle.com/forums/index.php?topic=55673.0 (accessed January 13, 2011).

Cogburn, R. (1993). A study of psychopathy and its relation to success in interpersonal deception. University of Oregon. 241 p. Retrieved from http://search.proquest.com/docview/304062569?accountid=6444

Collinson, D. (1988). Engineering humor: Masculinity, joking, and conflict in shop-floor relations. 9, 181-99.

Comte-Sponville, A. (2001). *A small treatise on the great virtues.* New York: Holt

Conran, P. (1989). *School superintendent's complete handbook: Practical techniques and materials for the in-service administrator.* Upper Saddle River, NY: Prentice Hall.

Cunningham, W. & Burdick, G. (1999). Empty offices. *American School Board Journal.* 186(12), 25-30.

Currie, W. (1973). Metaphors of alienation: The fiction of Abe, Becket, and Kafka. Doctoral dissertation. University of Michigan.

Cupitt, T. (2009). Tips on dealing with angry or difficult parents. *Principal Communicator.* At www.waterloo.k12.ia.us.

Czaja, M. & Harmon, M. (1997). Excessive school district superintendent turnover: An explorative study in Texas. *International Electronic Journal for Leadership in Learning.* 1(6).

Davidson, J. (1987). *The superintendency: Leadership for effective schools.* Jackson, MS: Kelwynn Press.

Deal, T., and K. Peterson. (1990). *The principal's role in shaping school culture*: Research in Brief. Washington, DC: Office of Educational Research and Improvement. At www.eric.ed.gov/ERICWebPortal/search/detailmini.jsp?_nfpb=true&_&ERICExt-Search_SearchValue_0=ED322618&ERICExtSearch_SearchType_0=no&acc-no=ED322618.

DeJONG (2007). DeJONG names top ten trends in school facility planning. At www.schoolfacilities.com/_coreModules/content/contentDisplay.aspx?contentID=2902 (accessed February 15, 2011).

Dimperio, J. (1996, March). Dealing with angry people: Brief article. *School Administrator.* At findarticles.com/p/articles/mi_m0JSD/is 3_53/ai_77195795/.

Donzelli, J. (2010, September 9). At last! Lee County School District bus audit released. At www.fox4now.com.

Downey, M. (2010, June 24). A letter to the new superintendent: Georgia has the lowest level of expectations . . . Get in the driver's seat. *Atlantic Journal Constitution.* At blogs.ajc.com/get-schooled-blog.

Dunbar, N., A. Ramirez, Jr., and J. Burgoon. (2003). The effects of participation on the ability to judge deceit. *Communication Reports* 16.

Duncan, H. E., & Stock, M. J. (2010). Mentoring and coaching rural school leaders: What do they need? *Mentoring & Tutoring: Partnership in Learning,* 18 (3), 293-311.

Dungca, N. (2010, August 17). West Linn-Wilsonville School District parents question superintendent Roger Woehl's retirement package. *Oregonian.* At www.oregonlive.com.

Dye, L. (2004). Study: First impressions really matter. ABC News. Retrieved from http://abcnews.go.com/Technology/Story?id=69942&page=1

Education indicators for the White House social statistics briefing room (SSBR). National Center for Educational Statistics, U.S. Department of Education. At nces.ed.gov/ssbr/pages/trends.asp.

Eisenhower, D. President Eisenhower quote. The Quotation Page. Retrieved from http://www.quotationspage.com/quotes/Dwight_D._Eisenhower

Enelow, W., & Boldt, A. (2006). *No-nonsense resumes: The essential guide to creating attention grabbing resumes that get interviews and job offers.* Franklin Lakes, NJ: The Career Press.

Fabiano, G. (2010, May 24). Leonia school chief holds sessions with parents over asbestos concerns. At www.northjersey.com.

Fiegehen, S. (1980). *First impressions: Their formation and implications for interpersonal processes in counseling.* University of Toronto (Canada). Retrieved from http://search.proquest.com/docview/303093295?accountid=6444

Fiore, T. (2004). *Taming the anger bee.* Angercoach.com. Retrieved from http://anger-coach.com/pdfs/Anger_Bee_0409.pdf

First meeting of superintendent's cabinet introduces goals, vision. (2010, August 7). *Americus (GA) Times-Recorder*. At americustimesrecorder.com.

Frank, D. (2002). Avoiding the peter principle: Promotion without pain. Cleanlink.com. Retrieved from http://www.cleanlink.com/ cp/article/Avoiding-the-peter-principle-promotion -without-pain--153.

Fullan, M. (2002). *Principals as leaders in a culture of change*. Ontario Institute for Studies in Education, University of Toronto. At www.michaelfullan.ca/Articles_02/03_02.pdf.

Fullan, M (2003). *The moral imperative of school leadership*. Thousand Oaks, CA.: Corwin Press.

Gibran, K. *Kahlil Gribran Apathy and empathy quotes*. Tentmaker.org. Retrieved from http://www.tentmaker.org/Quotes/apathy_empathy_quotes.html

Gifford, L. (2010). *Recruitment and retention of K-12 public school principals in a regional educational collaborative in Rhode Island*. Doctoral dissertation. Johnson and Wales University, Providence, RI.

Glass, F., L. Bjork, and C. Brunner. (2000). *The study of the American superintendency, 2000: A look at the superintendent in the new millennium*. Arlington, VA: American Association of School Administrators.

Glenn, J. (2008). *Superintendent search consultants' perceptions of school board candidates*. Doctoral dissertation, Sam Houston State University. At gradworks.umi.com/33/41/3341251.html.

Graf, L. (1996). *Superintendent burnout in the public schools: A study of demographic and environmental variables and their effects on the school superintendent*. Doctoral dissertation. University of La Verne.

Graham, B. Rev. Billy Graham quote. *Search Quotes*. Retrieved http://www.searchquotes.com/Billy_Graham/Sense_Of_Humor/quotes/

Greenleaf, R. K. (1977). *Servant leadership. A journey into the nature of legitimate power and greatness*. Mahwah, NJ: Paulist Press.

Gutloff, K., ed. (1966). *Building parent partnerships*. West Haven, CT: National Education Association Professional Library.

Heathfield, S. (2011). Performance appraisals don't work. At humanresources.about.com/od/performanceevals/a/perf_appraisal.htm (accessed January 13, 2011).

Henderson, E. (2003). Advice for retaining legal counsel: Guidelines for the superintendent and board members. *Journal of School Public Relations* 24(3), 199–211.

Heylighen, R. (2000). *Research in organizations: Foundations and methods of inquiry* (Ed. R. Swanson & E. Holton lll). San Francisco, CA: Berrett-Koehler.

Hill, F. (2005). *Educational facility master planning*: A 10-point check list for educational excellence. At www.schoolfacilities.com/_core Modules/content/contentDisplay.aspx?contentID=1926 (accessed February 15, 2011).

Hoekstra, E., Bell, A., & Peterson, S. (2008). *Humility in leadership: Abandoning the pursuit of unattainable perfection*. In Executive Ethics: Ethical Dilemmas and Challenge for the C-Suite (Edited by Quatro, S., and Simms, R.). Information Age Publishing.

Hoyle, J., L. Bjork, V. Collier, and T. Glass. (2005). *The superintendent as CEO: Standards-based performance*. Thousand Oaks, CA: Corwin Press.

Howard, M. (2002). *Perceptions of isolation among Georgia high school principals*. Doctoral dissertation. Georgia Southern University.

Houston, P. (2008). *No challenge left behind*. Thousand Oaks, CA: Corwin.

Hutnik, I., and N. Dehaney, eds. (2007). *How the world's best-performing school systems come out on top*. McKinsey & Company.

Jaksec, C. (2005). *The difficult parent: An educator's guide to handling aggressive behavior*. Thousand Oaks, CA: Corwin Press.

Jorgenson, O. & Peal, C. (2008). When principals lose touch with the classroom. *Principal*. 87(4), 52-55.

Kaatz, S. A. (2007). *Dealing with angry hostile parents*. Forest River, IL: Lutheran Education Association.

Kedrosky, P. (2009). *Solving the Peter principle? One word: darts*. InfectiousGreed. Retrieved from http://paul.kedrosky.com/archives/2009/07/solving_the_pet.html.

Kinzinger, R. (2007). *Nine reasons to hold regular staff meetings: Even when you don't want to do so.* Bloomington, IL: Talon. At www.taloncompany.com.

Kouzes, J., & Posner, B. (2008). *The leadership challenge* (4th ed.). San Francisco, CA: Wiley.

LaMance, K. (2009). When can a school be sued? At www.legalmatch.com/law-library/article/suing-a-school.html.

Lang, J. (2000). Staff meetings. At meetingsnet.com/corporatemeetingsincentives/ (accessed August 31, 2010).

Lazear, E. (2004). The Peter principle: A theory of decline. *Journal of Political Economy,* 112(1), S141-S163.

Lazear, E. (2000). *The Peter principle: Promotions and declining productivity.* Retrieved from www.siepr.standford.edu/papers/pdf/00-04.pdf.

Liberal, KS, USD 480. *District policies.* At www.usd480.net/policies/preface.htm.

Lindle, J. (1989). What do parents want from principals and teachers? *Educational Leadership* 47 (2), 12–14.

Livingston, J. (2003). Pygmalion in management. *Harvard Business Review.* Retrieved from http://hbr.org/2003/01/pygmalion-in-management/ar/1

Mark Tow & Associates (2010). How to win a lawsuit. At www.slideshare.net/ginalyn61/how-to-win-a-lawsuit.

Mathison, E. (2010, June 6). Charges expected soon for inappropriate physicals, Highline superintendent tells angry parents. *Highline Times.* At www.highlinetimes.com.

Mawhinney, L. (2008). Laugh so you don't cry: Teachers combating isolation in schools through humor and social support. *Ethnography and Education,* 3(2), 195-209.

McCarthy, P. (2011). Lawsuit prevention. *American School Board Journal* 198(9), 42–43.

McEwan, E. (1998). *Dealing with parents who are angry, troubled, afraid, or just plain crazy.* Thousand Oaks, CA: Corwin Press.

McGinnis A. *Alan Loy McGinnis quotes.* Quotesea.com. Retrieved from http://www.quotesea.com/quotes/by/alan-loy-mcginnis

Message to Voters (2011). At www.unionps.org (accessed February 14, 2011).

Michel, J. (2009). *Finding meaning in the midst of hardship.* Grand Forks Air Force Base. Retrieved from http://www.grandforks.af.mil/news/story.asp?id=123136729

Miller, B. (2008). *The uses and effects of humor in the school workplace.* Doctoral dissertation. University of Oregon. *ProQuest Dissertations and Theses,* Retrieved from http://search.proquest.com/docview/304487597?accountid=6444

Moody, A. (2007, August 31). Angry parents told district must focus on future. *Arizona Republic.* At www.azcentral.com.

Moore, M. (2010). *Reactions to job evaluations.* At www.ehow.com/about_6298299_reactions-job-evaluation.html (accessed January 13, 2011).

NAEP Overview. *National Assessment of Educational Progress.* National Center for Educational Statistics, U.S. Department of Education. At nces.ed.gov/nationsreportcard/about/.

Natkin, G., Cooper, B., Alborano, J., Padilla, A., & Ghosh, S (2002). *Predicting and modeling superintendent turnover.* Paper presented at AERA, New Orleans. Retrieved from http://www.eric.ed.gov.zeus.tarleton.edu:81/ERICDocs/data/ericdocs2/content _ storage_ 01/0000000b/80/27/8e/5b.pdf

New York superintendent wrestles gun away from angry parent. (2010, October 18). At www.ksdk.com.

Norton, M., L. Webb, L. Dlugosh, and W. Sybouts. (1996). *The school superintendency: New responsibilities, new leadership.* Boston: Allyn and Bacon.

O'Donovan, E. (2007, September). Dealing with difficult people: They can help clarify your mission. At www.districtadministration.com/viewarticle.aspx?articleid=1271.

Peter, L. & Hull, R. (1969). *The Peter principle.* New York: National General.

Pickhardt, C. (2003). Why parents get angry. At www.adoption.com.

Pluchino, A., Rapisarda, A., & Garofalo, C. (2009). The Peter principle revisited: A computational study. *Physica A,* 389, 467-72.

Powell, J. (2003). *A development of conceptual framework for principal evaluation and comparison of the framework to evaluation formats currently utilized in seven southeastern states.* University of South Florida. Retrieved from http://search.proquest.com/docview/304561818?accountid=6444

Public Schools of North Carolina. (2008). *North Carolina school executive principal evaluation.* State Board of Education, Department of Public Instruction. At www.ncptsc.org/Principal%20Evaluation%20Booklet%20-%20Fill%20In%20Forms.pdf.

Quito, A. (2009). *Art at work: Potential contributions of an art collection to non-profit organizations.* Masters Thesis. Georgetown University. Retrieved from http://search.proquest.com/docview/304887823?accountid=6444

Rabin, M., and Schrag, J. (1999). First impressions matter: A model of confirmatory bias. *The Quarterly Journal of Economics.* 114(1). 37-82.

Ramirez, A., Jr. (2004, September 7). Study: First 10 minutes after meeting may guide future of relationship. At researchnews.osu.edu/archive/1stimpre.htm.

Ray, J., I. Candoli, and W. Hack. (2005). *School business administration: A planning approach.* 8th ed. Boston: Pearson Education.

Redalen, E. (2010). *The survival guide for Iowa school administrators.* Iowa School Administrators. At resources.sai-iowa.org/.

Reeves, D. (2004). *Accountability in action: A blueprint for learning organizations.* Englewood, CO: Advanced Learning Press.

Renchler, R. (1992). *Student motivation, school culture, academic achievement: What school leaders can do.* At eric.uoregon.edu/pdf/trends/motivation.pdf.

Richards v. School Dist. of City of Birmingham, 83 N. W. 2d 643 (Michigan 1957).

Riggo, R. (2010). Do the incompetent rise to the Top? Peter principle revisited. *Psychology Today.* Retrieved from http://www.psychologytoday.com/blog/cutting-edge-leadership/201004/do-the-incompetent-rise-the-top-peter-principle-revisited

Roberts, R. (2010, August). *Interview on anatomy of a lawsuit.* Richey-Roberts Law Firm, Pryor, OK.

Roberts, R. (2011). *Standard practices.* Ritchie-Roberts Law Firm. Pryor, OK

Roberts, R. (2011). *How to win a lawsuit.* Ritchie-Roberts Law Firm. Pryor, OK.

Robinson, J., Horan, L., & Nanvati, M. (2009). Creating a mentoring coaching culture for Ontario school leaders. *Adult Learning,* 20(7), 35-38.

Rosberg, J., M. McGee, and J. Burgett. (2007). *What every superintendent and principal need to know.* 2nd ed. Gordon Burgett.

Russellville, Arkansas, board policies on facilities management. (2010). At rsdweb.k12.ar.us/schoolb/schoolbef.htm (accessed May 24, 2010).

Russo, C. J. (2004). *Reutter's the law of public education.* 5th ed. New York: Foundation Press.

Ryan, K. (2011, August 17). Joplin school term opens on time, major-hiccup free. *Joplin (MO) Globe.* At www.joplinglobe.com/local/x15272132/Joplin-school-term-opens-on-time-major-hiccup-free (accessed August 18, 2011).

Sampson, P. (2011). Chair of Superintendent Program. Stephen F. Austin State University. Nacogdoches, TX.

Sawaya v. Tucson High School Dist., 281 P.2d 105 (Arizona 1955).

Schultz, B (2005, June). Finally a superintendent: Now what? *The School Administrator,* 6(82). At www.aasa.org/SchoolAdministratorArticle.aspx?id=8506.

Seligman, M. (2000). *Conducting conferences with parents of children with disabilities.* New York: Guilford Press.

Siow, A. (1991). Are first impressions important in academia. Journal of Human Resources. 26(2).

Sixty-six percent of Texas schools meet AYP. (2011, August 4). At www.tea.state.tx.us/news_release.aspx?id=2147502010 (accessed August 19, 2011).

Smart Technologies editors (2004). What your meeting means to the CEO. *EffectiveMeetings.com.* Retrieved from http://www.effectivemeetings.com/meetingbasics/ceo_expectations.asp

Sovine, D. (2009). First year: Challenges and mediating strategies for novice superintendents. Unpublished doctoral dissertation.

Spears, L. (2005). *The understanding and practice of servant leadership.* School of Leadership Studies. Regents University.

Stone, C. (2005). *Management courage: Having the heart of a lion.* HRhero.com. Retrieved from http://blogs.hrhero.com/resources/2009/02/11/ management-courage-having- the heart of a lion/

Stout, L. (2010). *Superintendent questionnaire.* Liberal, KS: Liberal USD 480.

Sultanoff, S. (1995). Using humor in crisis situations. *Therapeutic Humor,* 12(5), 1-2.

Sultanoff, S. (1995). What is humor? At http://aath.org/articles/art_sultanoff01.html.

Susa, A. (2000). *Humor type, organizational climate, and outcomes: The shortest distance between an organization's environment and the bottom line is laughter.* Doctoral dissertation. University of Nebraska, Lincoln.

Sutton, S. (2008). Teachers' and administrators' perceptions of teacher evaluation. Doctoral dissertation, Wilmington College (Delaware).

Ten steps to pass a bond issue. (2011). At www.scholastic.com (accessed January 14, 2011).

Thomas, J. (2010). Search executives offer advice to superintendent seekers. At www.aasa.org.

Thompson, B. (2010). *Resume tips.* URLeader.com. [http://urleaderline.com]

Tizon, R. Robert Tison quotes and sayings. Searchquotes.com Retrieved from http:// www.searchquotes.com/quotes/author/Robert_Tizon/

Tobak, S. (2009, January 16). How to run an effective staff meeting. At www.cbsnews.com/ 8301-505125_162-28241647/how-to-run-an-effective-staff-meeting/

Union Public Schools (2011). Frequently asked questions. At www.unionps.org (accessed February 14, 2011).

Valente, W. (1994). *Law in the schools.* 3rd ed. Columbus, OH: Prentice-Hall.

Vecchio, R., J. Justin, and C. Pearce. (2009, Summer). The influence of leader humor on relationships between leader behavior and follower outcomes. *Journal of Managerial Issues* 21(2), 171–94.

Washington State Department of Health (2003). *How to run an effective meeting.* Olympia, WA: Office of Health Promotion.

Wasmund, B. *Bonnie Jean Wasmund Apathy and empathy quotes.* Tentmaker.org. Retrieved from http://www.tentmaker.org/Quotes/apathy_empathy_quotes.html

Wasser, J. (2009). *I'm calling my lawyer: A superintendent details his prudent policies and diligent follow up for reducing costly lawsuits against the school district.* The Gale Group, Education.com. (Retrieved from http://www.education.com/reference/article/aposiaposm-calling-lawyerapos-superintendent/] .

Waters, J. & Marzano, R. (2006). *School district leadership that works: The effect of superintendent leadership on student achievement.* Denver, CO: McREL

Wilkinson, B. (2001). Bud Wilkinson Quotes. *All Famous Quotes.com.* Retrieved fromhttp:// www.all-famous-quotes.com/Bud_Wilkinson_quotes.html

Wilson, R. L. (1993). A study of current practices of evaluation of the building principal in the state of Arkansas. Doctoral dissertation, University of Arkansas, Fayetteville.

Wise, V. (2011). *Telling our own story: Women and leadership in the early childhood setting.* Doctoral dissertation. George Washington University.

Wright, E. (2010, August 22). Location, location, location: Parents, superintendent exchange words over pre-K placement. *Hudson Reporter.*At www.hudsonreporter.com.

Xu, Shuli (2001). Teacher evaluation and student learning: Perceptions of elementary school principals and teachers. Doctoral dissertation, University of Massachusetts, Amherst.

Yen, G. (2003). Dressing for success. *Back Stage.* 44(34). A13-A14.